N O V A
B O O K

D1554876

Knoxville's
'Merry-Go-Round,'
Ciderville and...
the East Tennessee
Country Music Scene

by Ruth White

*This and the cover version adapted from an original print
by artist-musician Billy Robinson*

Nashville, Tennessee
(For a complete list of Nova Books titles,
check out **www.novabooksnashville.com***)*

Knoxville's
'Merry-Go-Round,'
Ciderville and....
the East Tennessee
Country Music Scene

Catalog data:
White, Ruth B. (Author)
With Foreword by Perry, James A.
Library of Congress Control
ISBN: 978-0-9908105-3-7 (pbk;softcover;alk.paper)
ISBN: 978-0-9908105-4-4 (e-bk.)
p.cm series (American Arts Culture)

First Printing

DEDICATION:

This book is dedicated to the many great musicians who performed on the stages of WNOX's Mid-Day *Merry-Go-Round* and The *Tennessee Barn Dance* in Knoxville, Tennessee. These hard-scrabble road warriors traveled over one hundred thousand miles a year, earning little money, just to entertain us and bask in the joy of making music.

They traveled the land in tired automobiles; negotiating secondary highways that today's motorist would never consider using. Their vehicles could be easily identified by the oversized "doghouse" bass strapped to their cars' roof, a trunk so full of guitars and other necessities that the elevated headlights resembled aircraft searchlights and by the exhausted occupants, whose profuse sweating - due to elevated summer temperatures - caused the windows to fog.

In addition, I dedicate this to all the great musicians who entertained us on WROL-Knoxville and at the Ciderville location, and to those who struggle to keep that venue alive and well. I salute you all!

Ruth White

WROL Country Playhouse participants (from left) an unknown announcer, with musicians L. E. White, Howard White, Roy Sneed, Ralph Cornish, Luke Brandon, on Knoxville's premier country telecast (1952).

PRELUDE

Nashville is only about one hundred and eighty miles from Knoxville, so it is easy to understand why musicians frequently made the four-plus hours drive west to *Music City*. My late husband, Howard White, and I often stopped in Knoxville, while traveling east from Nashville to his boyhood home in Charlotte, North Carolina. (Of course, we always made it a point to stop for lunch at the locally famous Regis Restaurant.)

Early in his career, Howard had played steel guitar on a WNOX-Knoxville radio show called *The Mid-Day Merry-Go-Round.* He loved to make me laugh with tales about the music and people in his life during this period. Through Howard, I developed a fascination with the culture, music and beauty of the East Tennessee city.

As rich and enjoyable as the music scene in Knoxville became, it was Nashville that developed into the heart of the industry. As such, Howard and I established careers there in different areas of the industry: Howard as a popular guitarist for more than two decades and later a successful song-plugger for top music producers; I worked for and managed publishing companies for over three decades, and then began a career as an author and researcher on music topics.

Not long ago, James Perry, a veteran radio personality, asked if I would be interested in writing a book about the history of the Knoxville music scene and specifically Howard's old show, the *Merry-Go-Round?* With the wealth of musical talent linked to the area, and remembering Howard's humorous anecdotes, I eagerly accepted the challenge.

Now this work required extensive research (and interviews), concerning the lives and careers of the many East Tennessee artists whose stories I have attempted to summarize in the pages that follow. I hope and I truly believe that you will find these profiles as interesting and compelling as I do. It is my great privilege to open the musical door to this rich, neglected and largely forgotten past.

Ruth White

FOREWORD
By James A. Perry

Ruth White's mentoring of me started some years ago, when I was led to her by Dr. John Simon of Portsmouth, Ohio, a country music historian and artist himself. "Miss Ruth" has organized, managed and tolerated almost everyone from the songwriters, publishers and recording studio personalities to the very top names at the music labels and the great artists themselves.

When Johnny Cash sang about "The Ways Of A Woman In Love," he certainly describes the love of the "real country" country music of yesterday by the author of this great book, Ruth White. She compiled accurate accounts of information by interviewing the few people still alive, who were there as sidemen and personalities. Although this was exhausting, from the gleam in her eyes, it was very enjoyable. Miss Ruth was in her element.

White has written numerous books on country music and Rhythm & Blues personalities, but this book takes you back to the beginning and ending of the venues that gave poor, rural entertainers and musicians their start in Knoxville, Tennessee, in the 1930s through the 1960s. From Roy Acuff to David West, this publication covers it all.

I am a simple radio show host on WNTT-AM (1250), Tazewell, Tennessee, but feel privileged to have assisted Miss Ruth in my small way, along the lengthy path to completion of such an informative and entertaining history of our late and great classic country music.

Ciderville Music Store exterior.

*Ciderville Music Store interior with (from left) James Perry,
Barb Edds, unknown picker and David West.*

CONTENTS:

INTRO - IN THE BEGINNING

"From the mountains and beyond,
They brought nothing but their songs."

Few people in America have been so romanticized, discussed and analyzed as these mountain folk who generally settled in the Southern Appalachian Mountains of the United States. They have been described as hardworking, independent, self-reliant and fiercely honest people. They came from Tennessee, the Carolinas, Georgia or Kentucky and were the most independent and self-reliant people anywhere. After their work in the fields and day was done, they played their fiddles, strummed their banjos, danced and sang around their fireplaces or pot-bellied stoves. It just came natural to them. Grandpa played an instrument and so did Daddy, Mama, and the kids sang and danced. Sons and daughters learned from their parents. Life was not easy in those rural areas. It was the worst of times, compared to our day of modern conveniences, but it was the best of times as radio had appeared on the horizon. WNOX-Knoxville decided to use these naturally talented rural musicians to add to their programming. They hired a man originally from Palmer, Illinois, to go into the mountains and look for talent. What he found began one of the most popular of radio shows, called *The Mid-Day Merry-Go-Round*. Soon to follow was *The Tennessee Barn Dance*.

Many, many artists got their start at WNOX, beginning in 1938. Future stars like Roy Acuff, Carl Smith, Bill Carlisle, Chet Atkins and so many more, found a home there on that Knoxville station. Some stayed longer than others, but they saw their amateur status turn to that of professional, under the guidance of Lowell Blanchard. Those two shows gave them the leg-up needed to boost promising careers. Indeed it was Lowell Blanchard who created the *Merry-Go-Round*. And it was good! Thus the boys and girls in the mountains came together, sometimes left and came together in other places; however, all good things come to an end. In 1962, with the popularity of rock and roll, WNOX changed its format to Top Forty sounds. By 1963, the era of the *Merry-Go-Round* and *Tennessee Barn Dance* ended at WNOX.

Then along came a man by the name of David West, who started a cider business where he made real apple cider and advertised: "Home Made Cider - Sweet, Sharp and Extra Sharp." He built a big bar to have a place for his patrons to drink his cider and "shoot the breeze." David played guitar and soon other entertainers stopped by with their instruments and they all had a great time pickin' and singin' together. Then people started coming by just to hear all that music.

"The nicest girl I ever saw / Was sippin' cider, through a straw / And now I've got a Maw-in-Law / From sippin' cider through a straw . . ."

It got so there was no place to sit. If the weather was bad, they had to shut down, so David, ever the entrepreneur, decided to build a music barn behind the Cider Mill Bar. It was a beautiful spot with a creek running behind, and he began building in October 1965; however, due to inclement weather, it wasn't ready for operation until August 1966. Opening night had to be expanded to two shows to accommodate so many musicians. At last the players from the hills and countryside had a stage to perform on once again.

In turn, people from miles around came to hear these performers, and as the crowds grew, so did his *Music Barn*. David West extended the barn's size by building on, even across the creek running behind it. Of course, the creek provided a natural air-conditioning, and today the creek still runs beneath the barn, and it's now called Ciderville. The location is ideal, situated in the Claxton community on Highway 25-West. Down the road is the trailer park where legendary Don Gibson once lived. Close by is the property containing the club or roadhouse where Gibson and his band had worked.

The Mid-Day Merry-Go-Round has almost faded from memory now, but David West still runs Ciderville. And that's good, giving the folk from the hills and hollows a stage to perform on, while sharing a mutual love of real country music with all who come for the entertainment. So it was, for decades, that all roads led to Knoxville's *Mid-Day Merry-Go-Round*, and then to Ciderville, as well.

"Play me some mountain music
Like my Grandma and Grandpa used to play . . ."

Excerpted from Alabama's Grammy Award-winning
song "Mountain Music," by Randy Owen.

People pack the January 25, 1937 broadcast of WNOX-Knoxville's
'Mid-Day Merry-Go-Round' (above) in the station's downtown auditorium
at 110 Gay Street, which boasted a capacity of about six hundred.

PART ONE

OUR APPALACHIAN HERITAGE

*"Fiddle sounds and blue tick hounds,
and the smell of country ham
in an iron skillet; and the soft haze
of the Great Smoky Mountains . . ."*

WNOX-Knoxville entrance to the Gay Street studio, where outside pictures plug performers inside.

1 BLAZING THE TRAIL TO KNOXVILLE . . .

"From time to time in life
You should sit tall on your horse
And look back over the trails
That those before you have traveled."

Old Indian Proverb.

Everything has its beginnings; so did the music of East Tennessee. The music we knew as "hillbilly" and later as "country," really began in the 17th century when the people of England, Ireland, Wales and Scotland made a great migration to the New World.

It was land that caused these first settlers to come here. They wanted to be free of the powers that oppressed them. They brought with them treasures of memory: old world folk tales, tragic ballads, love songs and rhymes, and a personal kind of religion. Their speech stayed alive in the hill country of Appalachia and beyond. Some of their earliest songs were ballads about King William of Orange. Those who sang them became known as "Billy boys" of the hill country or "Hillbillies."

The fiddle was of major importance in their jigs and reels. In the later half of the 1880s, the guitar was added. These mixes became very important to what we think of as country music today.

It seems likely that music was the greatest and most lasting contribution of the Scot-Irish people. They brought with them the mixture of Scottish and Irish music which is still characteristic of large parts of Northern Ireland. The distinctive "drone" notes of some modern day country music can be traced directly back to those original Scot-Irish people. That drone sound originally came from their bagpipes. They had to leave their bagpipes behind in the old country, but they were adept at imitating that sound on their fiddles and in their harmonies.

Eastern Tennessee, near the North Carolina border, is a world of forests, mountains and rivers. In the springtime that world is full of dogwood trees, Forsythias, Azaleas, Rhododendrons, mountain laurel and daffodils. Into all this beauty, over the rivers and through the woods, James White arrived and began a settlement he called White's Fort. He crossed the mountains to claim land which has been given him by the state of North Carolina in recognition of his service in the American Revolution. White's ancestors were originally from the lowlands of Scotland, later moving to County Londonderry, Ireland. They left Ireland in 1741, moving to Pennsylvania, then to Virginia and then to North Carolina

White arrived in what is now Knoxville in 1786. His land was located on the north bank of the Holston River, about four miles below the mouth of the French Broad River. In those days, the rivers were the settler's high-

1

ways. White built his house of logs with three rooms and a sleeping loft. He called it White's Fort. He also built a small mill to grind corn that he called White's Mill. Adjoining that was his turnip patch.

This tiny settlement began blossoming into a town when the Territorial Governor William Blount arrived. Blount built a two-story frame house, possibly the first frame house west of the Appalachias. In October 1791, Blount gave White the task of laying out a town they agreed to call Knox Ville, in honor of Major Henry Knox, the U.S. Secretary of War. When the state of Tennessee was formed in 1796, "Knoxville" became its first capital. Then James donated the land which held his turnip patch for the building of Knoxville's first Presbyterian Church. He and William Blount are both buried in the cemetery there.

More people followed, including settlers from Germany, and thus they began coming to our mountains, those strong willed people who forged their homes out of the wilderness and brought their love of music with them. The skills of the musicians who gathered there have passed their heritage on from generation to generation. They blazed the trail to Knoxville and set the stage for our musical history that followed. The WNOX *Mid-Day Merry-Go-Round* could not have existed without the music the mountain people brought with them.

Radio became popular in the 1920s and at that point hillbilly music suddenly became a business. Everybody that could hold a fiddle, banjo or guitar, and had knowledge of old-time tunes wanted to get into the act.

In 1924, Ernest (Pop) Stoneman first recorded "(The Sinking Of) The Titanic" for Ralph Peer, then at OKeh Records. During the first week of 1927, Peer, by then at Victor Records, journeyed to Bristol, a divided town partly in Tennessee and partly in Virginia, mainly to record local talent from surrounding areas.

Ralph Peer was one of the few New Yorkers familiar with Hillbilly music. Before Bristol, he had recorded a rural string band. After the session, he wanted to know the name of their band, and one of the musicians supposedly said, "Call us what you want to. We're just hillbillies from Tennessee." Peer took his cue and called them The Hillbillies, and the name stuck. Peer cut Pop Stoneman, known for his earlier hit "(The Sinking Of) The Titanic," and unknowns Jimmie Rodgers, and The Carter Family (A.P., Sara and Maybelle) along with others from in and around Bristol. These Southern acts made a great impact on what was to become Country Music. They had one foot in the past and one foot in the future.

Stoneman remembered Peer's crew arriving at Bristol with a couple of recording engineers and about twenty-five truckloads of equipment. They put carpet on the floor and to get the right acoustics they hauled carpet up with a big wooden block in the middle of it and made like a tent to encompass the sound. This supposedly would kill noises and echo in the building (it didn't). Engineers at the Bristol Sessions were Edward Eckhardt and Frank Lynob. That make-shift studio was at 408 State Street in the old Christian Hat Building on the Tennessee side.

Thus Country Music or Hillbilly developed in the South. The story-telling elements in their ballads are as strong and dominant now as they once were. The modern Southern writers' songs still have that Scot-Irish appeal. Dolly Parton, who boasts roots in the Smoky Mountains, has strong Scot-Irish blood in her veins, which always shows up in her songs. Jim McCarroll, one of the great old-time fiddlers, is still remembered in the mountains, having played all the old-time tunes like "Green River March" and "The Knoxville Girl."

"I met a little girl in Knoxville/A town we all know well/And every Sunday evening/Out in her home I'd dwell . . ." - Traditional.

Old mountain tunes were brought to light over and over. "Knoxville Girl" is a folk song derived from the Irish ballad "The Wexford Girl," which itself was inspired by the Elizabethan era broadside "The Cruel Miller." Although there are versions by later artists like the Louvin Brothers and the Wilburn Brothers, it is a song handed down through many singers and there are many versions and verses. (For instance The Blue Sky Boys, Bill and Earl Bolick, recorded a 1937 version as "The Story Of The Knoxville Girl.")

In 1958, a young man named Dave Guard found an old mountain tune "Tom Dula," written by poet Thomas Land. The ballad told of a nineteenth century North Carolina murder by former Confederate soldier Thomas C. Dula, who supposedly murdered his pregnant fiancee Laura Foster in May 1866. Dula was hung for the crime and protested to the end that he wanted everybody to know that "I didn't harm a single hair on that lady's head." Guard arranged it as "Tom Dooley" and the group of which he was a member, The Kingston Trio, recorded it on Capitol and it became a smash hit.

"Hang down your head Tom Dooley/Hang down your head and cry/ Hang down your head Tom Dooley/Poor boy, you're bound to die . . ."

Modern day country music may stray from their roots, but as Ricky Skaggs said, "Traditional country music has a warmth other music doesn't have. It's our roots, our heritage, it's everything we're about."

It was a short distance from Bristol to Knoxville. The backwoods country town of Knoxville grew from a "trifling town" into a thriving metropolis. So did WNOX rise from its fledgling beginnings to a station to be reckoned with, one of the ten oldest stations in the country, and it became a powerhouse in the entertainment industry.

"They were the ones when they crossed the sea,
To the land of hope and dreams,
Salute them now, whom none could cow,
Nor hold in light esteem.
Whose footsteps far in peace and war,
Still sought the setting sun,
With a dauntless word,
And a long bright sword,
The twain whom God made one."

The Reverend E. F. Marshall,
County Tyrone, Ireland.

2 WNOX...
The 'Mid-Day Merry-Go-Round'

"Throw down your dish-towel
Grab your easy chair
Let your housework wait awhile
If you're at the office,
Take your secretary on your knee
The crowd will teach you how to smile
Six minutes after noon, six days a week
Nine-ninety on your dial will be found
Just turn up the volume on your old radio
and hear 'The Mid-Day Merry-Go-Round.'"

Courtesy Robert K. Myrick

In the 1920s radio was still a novelty. Rural people listened in on their battery-operated radios. Ads appeared in the daily newspapers where you could send away for a crystal set you could build for a few dollars that was capable of bringing in stations from many miles away.

In November 1921 when sixteen-year-old Knoxville native Stuart Adcock first signed on the air, WNAV became the eighth station in the United States to come into existence. Radio was in its experimental stage. In 1924, that station burned to the ground. It returned in 1925 under direction of Peoples Telephone & Telegraph, and its call letters were changed to WNOX.

Adcock applied to the U.S. Department of Commerce to change the W to a K for Knoxville, but was refused. Regulations then stated stations west of the Mississippi River were to start with K and east of the Mississippi would start with a W. So WNOX it remained.

WNOX was a pioneer in broadcasting, not only for East Tennessee but for the entire region. The air-waves were so uncluttered at that time, WNOX could even be heard in New York City, when conditions were right.

Adcock sold WNOX in 1928 for three thousand dollars to the Sterchi Brothers, and it moved from the Saint James Hotel on Wall Avenue into the Andrew Johnson Hotel on Gay Street. In 1932, the brothers sold WNOX to the Liberty Life Insurance Company for fifty thousand dollars. Scripps-Howard Radio, Inc., next bought it for one hundred and twenty-five thousand dollars in 1934. (Scripps-Howard also owned the *Knoxville News-Sentinel* daily newspaper.)

From the start, broadcasting at WNOX consisted mostly of live productions. Their mission was to keep farm families up-to-date with new farming techniques, so they even staffed a farm director. He broadcasted in the early morning hours when farmers were getting ready to start their day. The farm director informed farmers how to get better yields from their crops and how to recycle their land. WNOX also stayed abreast of local news and kept in step with national news events as well. As a result, the station's power was increased to ten thousand watts, and soon became affiliated with the Columbia Broadcasting System (CBS) nationally.

R. B. (Dick) Westergaard was engaged as station manager and, in turn, he hired Lowell Blanchard in 1935, to drive into the hills and find talent for the station to audition. With a region like East Tennessee, untouched by pop culture, it was rich in a unique musical heritage.

Westergaard wanted to give a platform to local musicians. So Blanchard scoured hills and hollows, talking hillbilly performers he felt had talent into coming to Knoxville to try out on radio. Of course, this marked the beginning of two shows on the station: *The Mid-Day Merry-Go-Round* and later *The Tennessee Barn Dance*. People packed into the station to see these programs.

From the start, the *Merry-Go-Round* became the brainchild of announcer Blanchard, WNOX program director, who envisioned it as the best live hillbilly show in East Tennessee. That variety show featured local talent boasting a bit of everything. MGR had a big band, gospel music, hayseed comics and hillbilly bands and singers. The weekend *Tennessee Barn Dance* was exclusively dedicated to the new hillbilly sound Blanchard discovered and promoted enthusiastically.

From 1936 to 1961, the *Merry-Go-Round* and *Tennessee Barn Dance* were on the air. Their performers became heroes. MGR began at noon and ran until 1:30 p.m. six days a week. As the last band went off stage on Saturdays, they broke the set down and set up for the nightly *Barn Dance*. Blanchard was a great Master of Ceremonies. He could remember little details of where he found musicians and how he heard about them. He'd insert that into this stage patter, which made him a much-admired M.C. Indeed, Blanchard was a consummate showman, as well as a master of stage craft.

WNOX announcer Blanchard razzes pioneer brother duo Bill and Cliff Carlisle.

Lowell Blanchard also wrote his daily scripts to present on mic and developed a keen country sense of humor, learning the accent as well, and when he hit that stage he was ready for business. Historically, the *Merry-Go-Round's* first broadcast was live from the second floor of the Market House, right in the heart of downtown Knoxville's hillbilly music scene. So many wanted to see and hear these musicians that WNOX had to find a new and bigger venue, moving into the Andrew Johnson Hotel, up on the seventeenth floor.

That same year the MGR debuted from the top floor of the Andrew Johnson Hotel, as the crowds, which started as a trickle, gradually increased. Lines began forming around the block every day just before noon, as people were anxious to hear the music of these talented country artists. The high lonesome vocals and lightning-fast finger picking players attracted true fans to the studio sounds emanating from the hotel.

As noted earlier, these talents came straight off the farms and out of the mountains, raw music hopefuls who "sawed, picked, sang and joked" so naturally, just as they had back home. Mostly, the musicians were a slow-moving bunch inching their way through the hotel lobby, carrying fiddles, banjos, big bass fiddles, and crowding into the elevators. These hillbilly performers, some heard cussing as they jammed into crowded elevators, became an unwelcome sight to tourists. Guests complained so often - and it wasn't lost on management that the growing crowds caused traffic problems outside as well - that finally the powers-that-be asked the station to move out.

WNOX found another location at 110 Gay Street, which boasted an auditorium and a capacity of six hundred. When the station boosted its signal to ten thousand watts in 1937, WNOX dominated the air-waves throughout the region. The *Merry-Go-Round* became a noon-time institution for a generation or more of East Tennesseans and beyond. Meantime, it also proved a launching pad for performer with stars in their eyes.

Among the first to attain nationally-known names after their stints on the *Merry-Go-Round* were Roy Acuff and Homer & Jethro. Later, the likes of Bill Carlisle, Archie Campbell, Chet Atkins and The Carters joined the cast. Within months, Acuff was drawing crowds with his Crackerjacks band, later labeled The Crazy Tennesseans, but soon was auditioned by WSM-Nashville's *Grand Ole Opry*, where he had to change his band name to the more acceptable (to management) Smoky Mountain Boys before joining in 1938.

By 1940, WNOX was programming more country music than WSM-Nashville, for East Tennessee fans seem to have been more receptive to the hillbilly music style. Among WNOX's rural type comedians were sensational acts that proved a major draw for the two shows, including Archie Campbell and Bill Carlisle a.k.a. Hotshot Elmer. Then there was Ray Myers, who despite being armless, could play guitar with his feet, and who was such a unique entertainer he became a major attraction at the 1933 World's Fair in New York.

Yet another handicapped musician making his mark at MGR was Emory Martin, a one-armed banjoist, who wrapped a shirt around his six-inch stub on his left arm for rhythm pickin' while noting with his good right arm. He was recognized as a skilled guitarist, who performed with Johnnie & Jack in their early career.

When Cowboy Copas came on the scene, he brought Little Moses, the human lodestone. For some reason, nobody could lift him, though he only weighed ninety pounds, but he had devised a way to relax that made it almost impossible to get a grip on him. As Chet Atkins once stated, "At WNOX our claim to fame were the characters we had around."

Most radio shows in the 1940s were live, and WNOX had more than one hundred and fifty half-hour programs per week, most featuring country sounds. At one time, Johnnie & Jack, featuring Kitty Wells, had a morning program. When Jack Anglin departed to join the Army, Johnnie Wright teamed with singer-comic Eddie Hill. Young Chet Atkins played fiddle for them on the show and on the road, but at noon Chet played guitar on the *Merry-Go-Round.*

WNOX performers all used their station appearances to promote live shows coming up on the road, and in turn generously plugged the station during gigs, proclaiming when appropriate, *"Come one, come all! See your favorites from radio station WNOX in Knoxville, Tennessee. Tonight! In person!"* Their regional fame came from their radio performances, making possible bookings at rural schoolhouses, grange halls and churches throughout the listening area, covering East Tennessee, Virginia and North Carolina.

Music was enjoyable back then. When an artist landed a spot on the *Barn Dance* or *Merry-Go-Round,* they not only did it for the name recognition, but because it sounded like fun. They didn't think a lot about the money and that's just as well because they were paid very little. But many had been used to absolutely no money being paid back in the hills, where mostly they played for love of the music. So getting even a small sum, while having a professional venue to perform in, meant everything to these newcomers.

Often when farmers took a lunch break from their fields and chores around noontime, they tuned their radios into the *Mid-Day Merry-Go-Round*; though the music being broadcast traveled far beyond the hills. It was carried into the living rooms, work places and cars of people elsewhere. All of these same folk tuned into *The Tennessee Barn Dance* on Saturday night, for a big three-hour jamboree. Audiences at the station for these shows would be standing room only for the most part.

WNOX's local competition was station WROL-Knoxville, which also boasted morning shows featuring live entertainment. Both also offered weather, news and farm reports. Rivalry between the two stations was fierce, but friendly. Blanchard constantly tried to out-do Cas Walker at WROL. Cas was a local grocer who learned he could sell a lot of groceries via radio advertising. He was also a great fan of bluegrass music, calling it "jumpin' up and down music."

As a result, Walker gave a helping hand to Flatt & Scruggs and a ten-year-old Dolly Parton. Actually, Roy Acuff began at WROL before switching to WNOX, but came back again to WROL. That was not unusual in those days. Often musicians came to WNOX with one band, then leave with another, and maybe return in a different band.

Roy Acuff

The *Merry-Go-Round* became one of the nation's first continually running and very successful regional radio stations programming country music. The only time the station went off the air was a three-day hiatus in respect, following the death of President Franklin D. Roosevelt. WNOX's *Tennessee Barn Dance* also became part of the CBS *Saturday Night Country Style* program, broadcast nationally by the network.

As artists honed their talents, they came and went without much ceremony, but were always succeeded by equally promising acts. Sometimes a performer would exchange show costumes for their former overalls to concentrate on their personal life and start families, but at least for that sweet moment in the spotlight, they had been stars.

In 1954, WNOX bought the old Whittle Springs Resort & Hotel in north Knoxville, and then in 1958 relocated there from their long-time Gay Street site. The owner also built an auditorium at Willow Springs. It's also where reportedly Don Gibson wrote his classic song "Sweet Dreams."

After World War II, attendance at the *Merry-Go-Round* and *Barn Dance* began to decline. Then with the coming of television, the public's taste in music changed, and following the move to Willow Springs, the MGR show was canceled (1961). News of the cancellation was barely a blip in news reports. Two musicians on the last show were Jerry Collins and Tony Musco. Afterwards, Musco taught accordion students, while Collins and his orchestra worked regular gigs such as country clubs in the area.

In 1962, the station switched formats to Top Forty music. Still WNOX had become a legend in its own time, thanks to the people behind the mic who made it such a welcome visitor into the homes of so many music lovers of that era. Another part of its proud legacy was serving as something of a training ground - and home - to some of the genre's greatest talents, thanks to their heartfelt participation on both the *Merry-Go-Round* and *Barn Dance*.

For those, desiring to remember those good old days, there's a monument in Crutch Park, in the shape of a huge treble clef, to commemorate the legacy of Knoxville, having earned the title *Cradle Of Country Music,* alluding to the many rookie stars WNOX turned into legends in their own right. Nostalgically we can still recall the spiel, *"... Turn up the volume on your old radio, and hear the Mid-Day Merry-Go-Round ..."*

3 WNOX DJ...
Lowell Blanchard

"The *Merry-Go-Round* was the farm team for the Opry."

Mac Wiseman

Ace announcer Richard Lowell Blanchard, born November 5, 1910, in Palmer, Illinois, was the son of Betty (Priest) and Jay William Blanchard, a grocer, who for seventeen years was the city's mayor. Growing up, Lowell worked for his father and toughened himself up working at an area farm. He got into radio while attending the University of Illinois, and landed an enviable assignment as emcee during the 1933 Chicago World's Fair (the year he graduated).

Lowell had aspirations of being an actor, but broadcasting at stations in Indiana, Iowa and Michigan inspired him even more, and while program director at a Des Moines, Iowa, station, he hired young Ronald Reagan as a sports announcer (a man who actually did become an actor).

Reportedly when WNOX's Dick Westergaard hired him in January 1936, he said, "You are to become a hillbilly. Bring us hillbilly performers. Be one of them," which appealed to the actor in him. The station had already produced such raw talents as Mac & Bob, a harmonious duo (Lester McFarland and Bob Gardner), who first met at the Kentucky School For

Lowell Blanchard with (from left) Howard White, Luke Brandon, Minnie Pearl, Roy Sneed and L. E. White. Original 1951 picture hangs in Ciderville Museum. (Photo courtesy of Kathleen White.)

9

the Blind, and became fast favorites in 1920s Knoxville; Hugh Cross, who had his own program from 1926-'29; and Otis Elder & The Smoky Mountain Ramblers, whose program was sponsored by a Knoxville dentist.

In Blanchard's quest for as yet undiscovered entertainers, he developed an ear for good music and true talent, then persuaded the usually shy, often backward performers to come to Knoxville and learn to play before a big audience. An early sponsor was Scalf's Indian River Tonic. One of the first acts Lowell announced for and promoted was Acuff and his Crackerjacks, who had their own noon show launched the year before Blanchard came aboard. In March 1936, however, Acuff suddenly departed WNOX and filling that vacancy was the newly-created *Mid-Day Merry-Go-Round*, which soon boasted its own staff band called The Dixieland Swingsters. WNOX staff musicians have included such as Charlie Collins, multi-instrumentalist; Dave Durham and Harry Nides, fiddles; Jerry Collins, piano; Tony Musco, accordion; Chet Atkins and Sunshine Slim Sweet, guitars; and on bass Hubert Carter, who also served as station traffic director.

Blanchard wrote his radio scripts, hosted his own morning program *The Musical Clock,* and even featured a *Man On The Street* segment, heard just before noon, when if an alarm clock sounded during an interview, the subject chatting won five dollars. Lowell also did some singing, including an uptempo 1950 recording "Jesus Hits Like An Atom Bomb," with his Valley Trio.

What's more, Blanchard is credited with launching - or reinvigorating careers - of artists who became giants in the music business, including Archie (Grandpappy) Campbell, Homer & Jethro (whom he named, after they stepped out of their Stringdusters band), Kitty Wells (encouraging her to drop her real name, Muriel Deason), Martha Carson (whom he inspired to go it alone, after her divorce from duet partner James), Mother Maybelle and The Carter Sisters (who left, taking Chet Atkins with them), Bill Carlisle (who perfected his comedic talents, as brother Cliff split), Carl Smith (a Maynardville, Tennessee native), and Molly O'Day (who soon switched from country to gospel). Blanchard himself became a leading promotional voice in country music, and he had more of a fan following than many of the artists walking out on stage.

In addition he was kind to young, amateur artists and musicians seeking their first break in the business. In one instance, he attended a talent show in Athens, Tennessee, at North City School where he heard a duet by the Stewart Twins (Oneta Wright and Juanita McPeak). Lowell invited the duo to guest on the *Mid-Day Merry-Go-Round*. The twins remembered that night forever, recalling that Lowell Blanchard sang "My Blue Heaven" on that show. Later, Oneta took accordion lessons from Tony Musco. Both ladies now teach guitar, Oneta in Athens and Juanita in Springfield, Tennessee.

Blanchard also booked acts for shows in schoolhouses and theaters throughout the area, and sometimes accompanied them on the road. Sometimes performers would depart the *Merry-Go-Round* show, play a gig somewhere that night, return in the morning, park their cars near the studio, and catch a few winks in the vehicle until it was time to do a morning show.

Even as artists were getting ready to go on stage for the *Merry-Go-Round*, Blanchard might still be reviving a script, and thinking on how to make the show run smoothly. At the same time, Charlie Collins was probably revving up The Dixieland Swingsters, while Musco was likely doodling his accordion, and Sunshine Slim tuning his guitar for the first number scheduled. Seven-foot singing cowboy Homer Harris was prepping his vocals, and Claude Boone might have been practicing a new tune. Sidekick Charlie Pickel, no doubt was checking his song as part of the Archie Campbell troupe.

Bill Carlisle   George Riddle

Lowell (Smiley) Blanchard ran unsuccessfully for Mayor in 1963.

An SRO crowd of 600 waited impatiently for the show to commence, and emcee Lowell was responsible to make sure everyone backstage knew when and where to make their entrance and exits. According to his schedule, the show was divided into fifteen-minute segments. Other sponsors besides Scalf's included Red Ash Charcoal Company, and Planter's Peanuts. Blanchard could take credit assuring the auditorium benches were filled each day, many attending on their lunch break, others left their fields in the country, to see the show, along with visitors from farther afield.

It was in June 1942 that WNOX began its Saturday night *Barn Dance* in the Lyric Theater situated in the 700 block of Gay Street. Musicians and artists alike from the *Mid-Day Merry-Go-Round* joined numerous guest stars, drawn to the program when CBS incorporated it into their national broadcast schedule, alternating every other Saturday evening with the Richmond, Virginia-based *Old Dominion Barn Dance*.

As World War II progressed, radio station jobs opened up as staff members joined the military. Among the replacement announcers were Texas DJ Grant "Tex" Turner, who also doubled on the *Mid-Day Merry-Go-Round*, until the Solemn Old Judge George D. Hay "drafted" Tex for duty at WSM-Nashville. In retrospect, Turner remembered he was playing golf with Hay the day they learned President Roosevelt died at Warm Springs, Georgia, in April 1945.

The end of the war prompted a slow decline in attendance at the shows. As television began to take hold of the populace, it too cut into the crowd size. When WNOX moved its operation in 1958 to the suburbs, the audience didn't follow. Finally both shows were canceled in 1961. For a time, Lowell played recorded music in that time slot, but music tastes were also changing, due to the rise of rock and roll.

For awhile Blanchard remained at the station selling ad time, then in 1964, he resigned and concentrated on being emcee at horse shows and various sport events. He even became noted at baseball games for his "will he" lead-off line, like "Will he walk him?," and "Will he strike him out?" They say the apple doesn't fall far from the tree, so Lowell like his father before him, won two terms as city councilman and ran for mayor and state legislature, though unlike dad, lost.

Mac Wiseman, who in 1952 was working as a solo at WNOX, just loved Lowell Blanchard. Mac said, "Lowell was the Arthur Godfrey of country music. (Godfrey's *Talent Scouts* was a forerunner of *American Idol* and *The Voice*.) Blanchard handled the business, booking and comedy for his shows. The *Merry-Go-Round* was the farm team for the Opry."

According to Archie Campbell, "Lowell Blanchard was the best straight man I ever encountered." It is said that Blanchard's comedy routines on the *Merry-Go-Round* later were reincarnated on *Hee Haw*. (Campbell was in charge of comedy writing for *Hee Haw* routines.)

Blanchard also collaborated with John Ward providing on-air color for the University of Tennessee basketball team. Immediately after one such basketball game in January 1968, Blanchard, fifty-seven, suffered a heart attack. He died just after midnight on February 18, 1968. Upon learning of his death, some believed he died of a broken heart.

It was in April 1968, when artists and fans from across the country assembled in Knoxville's Civic Coliseum for a final *Mid-Day Merry-Go-Round* reunion farewell honoring Blanchard's great contribution to country music. Among attendees at this tribute were Roy Acuff, Kitty Wells and Johnnie Wright, Ramona and Grandpa Jones, Skeeter Davis and Don Gibson.

In 1977, the WNOX radio legend Lowell Blanchard was inducted into the Country Music Disc Jockey Hall of Fame by the Country Radio Broadcasters. He's hailed as the top announcer of all time,

Mac Wiseman

who served as a role model for generations of broadcasters, and is regarded as the first genuine on-air voice of East Tennessee.

4 CIDERVILLE ...
And David West

"Ring, ring the banjo
I like that good old song,
We'll tune the old piano
When the banjo's out of tune."

Stephen Foster

Today Ciderville is known for a fun Saturday night show, where real country music is still being played. To those who like the traditional sound, it takes the place of shows like *Mid-Day Merry-Go-Round* and *The Tennessee Barn Dance* that were so loved in the Knoxville area.

David West, a musician first and then a businessman – or maybe first a businessman and then a musician – started it all, just selling cider. It all began on old Highway 25-W, then a two-lane highway. My daughter Kathleen and friends, songwriter Gary Gentry and Shirley Hutchins, publishing administrator, were with me visiting the Roy Acuff Museum in Maynardville.

James Perry invited us to visit Ciderville on a Saturday night. We were amazed at the talent heard, playing music that it seems Nashville has forgotten, original sounds of the mountains and rural areas. Among the many fine artists heard that night was a twelve-year-old girl, Erin Ott, who sang a Patsy Cline number and a Patsy Montana song, even yodeling like the original Western hitmaker. There, too, was Rita Cianciola, whose brother and a cousin played originally on the *Merry-Go-Round*. Guitarist Jason (Rowdy) Cope played "Long Tall Texan," just like my late bass-playing friend Henry Strzelecki, who wrote it in 1959.

The man behind all this, David West, is himself an extraordinary banjoist. We wanted to know all about David. According to his sister Faye West, their mother was born in Bluefield, West Virginia, and their father was a Tennessean. Mom moved to Tennessee in about 1915, and met her future husband in church and after three years of courtship they were wed. Mr. West then worked for the L&N Railroad. The couple had two daughters Faye and Alma, and when the younger girl was twelve, David was born.

Checking out their genealogy, their great grandfather Edward West was born in 1816. After marrying Arminda Roberts, they lived in Knox County. In 1860, the Wests moved to Jefferson County. West was a staunch Union man and assisted carrying Confederate information to the Union Army during the Civil War. As a result, the Confederates burned out West's woodworking shop twice before he moved to Anderson County. He died in 1892.

David's great-grand uncle, Dr. Thomas A. West, born in 1841, studied medicine in New York City. Soon after, he entered military service for the Union Army. Afterwards, Dr. West practiced in Knox County, and was a

14

Knoxville City physician during the 1880s. He opened the Oliver Springs Drugstore in 1900, and died in 1923.

"No," David said, "We don't make cider anymore, but we still call this place Ciderville; however, we still sell R.C. Colas." Anxious to learn how all this came about, David related his story regarding Ciderville. He was born and bred in East Tennessee, where both parents were musicians, but in the main they were business people first. Dad taught him early in life, "Don't ever forget your upbringing."

David West learned to love music from a young age, but like many others in the area, he grew up doing exactly what he wanted to do, whether it was business or music, never forgetting his upbringing. At age five, he listened intently to Carl Story and his Rambling Mountaineers on the radio, and from then on he strived to play the guitar. Initially he grabbed his mother's broom and began strumming on it, playing it like a guitar. Having heard Carl say at show's end, "Goodbye now, we'll be here again tomorrow," the mystified youngster, unclear as to how those voices got into that radio, asked, "Where do they go to?" Mother replied, "Why they go to their homes."

David told how as a six year old he watched the widening of Highway 25-W in front of their farmstead. The road laborers would warn all the families in the homes about the times that they were going to blast: "Bring your kids home, get them inside and cover their heads!"

Faye West and brother David at Ciderville.

David attended Claxton Elementary School, six miles from the Knoxville city limits. There were eight classrooms, a gymnasium and an outhouse. A pot-bellied stove provided the only heat. Even back then David was developing a business-like mind, buying Pop-Right Popsicles, saving the coupons printed on back, and redeemed them for a cowboy belt and pocket knife. He swapped the knives for notebook paper and pencils.

In 1950, David traded for a real lunchbox, after years of carrying lunch in paper "pokes" (bags). David said he learned to drive at age eight, standing on the seat, steering, while Dad actually controlled the clutch, gas pedal and brake on their 1939 Dodge Truck. The family all attended church on Thursday, Saturday and Sunday.

After his coupon saving events, David's next venture was selling popcorn to the church crowd following services, calling after their trucks and cars, "Get your popcorn here!" Soon he was adding R.C. Colas to the spiel.

"I had the greatest Dad ever made," said David. "I went everywhere with him and the people seemed to love me." It was about 1950 that his father started building rabbit boxes. Then he would sell the trapped rabbits, going house to house. Starting with six of the creatures, they soon totaled thirty-six and their number increased even more.

It was his father who inspired David's business acumen. He remembered Dad filled their truck with corn and sold it out on the highway. Mr. West also sold corn to the grocers in the area. To get an early start, they would arise at five-thirty a.m. to sell the corn. During the winter, Dad sawed wood daily and hauled it out at night to sell. That work ethic stayed with David throughout his life.

Kids in the neighborhood hung out at David's house. It seems they all had bicycles that always seemed to need fixing. David kept his own bike running smoothly and also repaired theirs to earn a few dollars more. When he needed parts for repair, he located old bicycles rusting away in old barns, and agreed to haul them away just to get parts off them.

In his teens, David met Ova Abston from Texas, who had been a friend to World War I's most decorated hero, Sergeant Alvin York, a Tennessean. Abston had been painting signs, but wanted to rent a building from David's dad in which to sell his art. He came well-recommended by Cas Walker. While Abston did well sales-wise, he didn't feel he was making enough money doing that, so he built a place of slabs, and had his wife sell cider there. He asked David to work there for a dollar a day, selling cider. That did so well, they added R. C. Colas, and the business took off like a house afire. Mrs. Abston, who had been a sergeant in the Army, didn't like the cider business, so David sort of inherited their operation.

That original cider mill was a hand-cranked cider mill, until David revised it, putting an electric motor on it, made from a hydraulic auto motor jack. The mill had a two-gallon "hopper." Apples were hard to get, so Abston bought an immense trailer and purchased apples in Virginia. He put the cider into a crock, strained it into juice and let it ferment. His home-made sign proclaimed, *"Home Made Cider - sweet, sharp and extra sharp."* Although the cider began fermenting, he wouldn't use the term "hard" cider.

16

People came from everywhere. Even country singer Don Gibson became a customer and reportedly wrote "Oh Lonesome Me" while sipping cider. Then they built a big bar in front to accommodate people drinking cider and "shooting the breeze." In the winter naturally business fell off, so they started cooking beans and cornbread to attract customers. Some days they served hamburger chili or squirrel or rabbit stew.

Abston was a good artist, who did murals for *Holiday On Ice* shows, churches, and some of his creations can still be seen around Knoxville. David noted, "I learned a lot from Mr. Abston. I helped him paint signs, learning about stains, how to mix paints and how to spray paint. I got my education from people like him, selling cider and painting." When Mr. Abston left, going to Knoxville for his home and shop there, he advised David: "You ought to stay in this cider business on your own."

When David was sixteen in 1957, he became owner of that business. That next year white racist agitator Frederick John Kasper, from Camden, New Jersey, and Asa Carter, former Ku Klux Klan leader from Alabama, came into the area to speak in September 1958, mainly to protest integration of the high school ordered by a federal judge. Their hate speech inspired the October 5th bombing of Clinton High School, and everything was in disorder. A violent confrontation ended only when National Guard troops and tanks arrived for two months to stop the disruption. That fall, David quit school and went into the cider business full time.

One day a black man pulled up to get some cider, and asked David: "Why aren't you in school?" David said, "I quit!" The man said, "Oh no, you ain't got no future." After the man departed, David stood there thinking, "Everybody I get to know, I learn from. I watch them all and I learn." Possessing a great personality, David made a point to remember everyone's name and he learned. (When Ova Abston died in 2000, David spoke and played banjo at his funeral.)

Although David watched *The Cas Walker Farm & Home Hour* TV show, he would've loved advertising on his program, but couldn't afford it. So he made signs to put up on the side of the road, advertising his cider, and by this time was also selling bedspreads, rugs, chips and cold drinks, added to the mix.

In 1959, David's cousin started a floor-sanding business. When he wasn't selling cider, David helped him sand floors, learning that business as well. Like most businesses, it suffered its ups and downs, and in 1963, David quit the floor-sanding business. In 1964, he began driving a school bus, a part-time job, while continuing to run his cider mill. He drove the bus until 1969, for Clinton and Claxton.

He pointed out there was a really cute girl riding the bus, whom he wanted to get to know better. She explained that her father didn't allow her to date, but one day told him dad would be away and invited David to come see her. A delighted David drove his truck out to her house, but when he arrived saw her on the porch, motioning for him to drive off. Suddenly her dad appeared on the porch, shotgun in hand and said, "What do you want here?"

Spotting some pigs in the yard, the quick-thinking suitor replied, "I want to buy three of your pigs. I'll pay you two dollars a pig." David had three barrels in the back of his truck and put a pig in each barrel. On the ride home, he stopped to gas up and a farmer there asked, "Those are sure nice pigs you have there, wanna sell 'em?" David said, "I might." The farmer asked how much, and David told him five dollars each. Well, the farmer bought them and David pocketed fifteen dollars, making nine dollars profit. (And that's West's version of "The Three Little Pigs.")

At his cider mill, David began to diversify. He put in horseshoe pits, and soon had people waiting inline to play. He also added a turkey shoot which attracted people from miles around to shoot at targets and hopefully win a turkey or ham. Targets cost a dollar apiece, and David confided there may have been some gambling among the players, but he wasn't a part of that.

David had started playing guitar after hearing musicians on the radio, but when he heard Earl Scruggs, he just had to have a banjo. Then he picked up on the Ralph Stanley style of playing. It set him on fire, his sister said, remembering how he played "Cripple Creek."

Soon he was performing in a building on site, and people started stopping by to listen and other entertainers began coming by to play their instruments, as well. Then David got a flat-bed trailer and they used it as a stage, playing on that truck. Talk about crowds! These were some of the best years of David West's life, and he met many entertainers doing this, including David Farmer, who still helps put on shows at Ciderville.

David got really good at singing "Sippin' Cider Through a Straw." It happened that on crowded shows, there wasn't any place to sit and if the weather was inclement, they simply had to shut down. David took heed

WSM's first 'Grand Ole Opry' telecast in 1955 borrowed its merry-go-round theme from WNOX in publicizing its show, while depicting former Knoxville stars June Carter, Roy Acuff, Carl Smith and Martha Carson (among cast regulars such as Hank Snow, Ernest Tubb, Jimmy Dickens and Solemn Ol' Judge George D. Hay).

18

when he heard somebody exclaim, "It's a pity you haven't got a place for the audience to sit!"

So David decided, why not build a music barn? That led to him building that barn in October 1965, and it was the worst winter they had seen in years, so building had to stop until spring 1966. While waiting for the weather to clear, David talked the music barn idea over with Lowell Blanchard, who offered sound advice. West was building the barn with concrete floors, and Blanchard said that was great; guys could put their cigarette butts out on the floor.

"There are three kinds of people: the rich, the poor and the middle-class," said Lowell. "The rich will come to hear great music, and they can afford it. They can smoke and put their cigarettes out on the floor, as they aren't allowed to do that at home. The poor will come because it's their kind of music and they will do without something to be able to afford it. The middle class won't come because they are trying to live up to the rich with expensive houses and cars, and won't have the price for a hillbilly show."

On August 20, 1966, West opened his *Music Barn* for the first show. The head count was one hundred and forty-two, and they did two shows. David began charging fifty-cents each for the first show, 8-10 p.m. and fifty cents for the second, 10-12 p.m. After a few months, the ticket tab went up to a dollar. Still, all sorts of folk turned up to watch, sing or play, everything from bluegrass to country. There were even guest artists from WSM's Opry, including former Knoxville radio stars Roy Acuff and Bill Carlisle. Blanchard proved right, the rich and poor came to listen to the music and to dance.

David would construct another building where he also sold instruments and accessories such as guitar strings and picks, mostly selling used instruments, as well as trading instruments. By 1968, David had learned to play ten or twelve tunes on an old banjo, but he wanted a Gibson, which were hard to find back then. Then he heard that Jim Ball, former fiddler with the Osborne Brothers, had one for sale in Gatlinburg. So David and a buddy drove over to see Jim's Gibson Banjo. Unfortunately, they learned that Jim's banjo was tied up in a divorce settlement; however, Ball's band needed a banjoist and asked David to play with them. Although David didn't feel he was professional enough, Jim sweetened the deal by offering twenty dollars a night for one hour, and upping it to thirty dollars if he played two hours. So a reluctant West agreed to try it for a night.

That first night he played, he was surprised to see all the gals screaming for them when they performed, and enticed by the excitement of the crowd, David played their entire season. Playing nights left him free during the day to take care of business for Ciderville. Meanwhile, the band worked seven nights weekly at places like Fort Apache and Gold Rush Junction where Tom Woods emceed, and their show dates were promoted on WROL by Cas Walker. According to West, "We were pickin' ourselves to death."

When the season ended, David concentrated more on Ciderville. Noticing business was falling off, David acquired three big old trucks, filled them with rocks, painted "David's Ciderville" on the doors, and went from door to door asking folks to re-rock their driveways, but soon learned that truck insurance was too high.

Then along came Bonnie Lou & Buster, who heard David's pickin' at Beck's Circle-rama, a circus in which he had toured all over Tennessee and Kentucky. With their banjoist Bill Chambers departing, they asked David to drop by for a chat. At that time they were residing at Shiland Trailer Park near Ciderville, so David agreed to meet with them. When he drove up to her trailer, Bonnie Lou was raking leaves, and she invited him to play with her and Buster on Cas Walker's TV program, sponsored by Jim Walter Homes.

David figured it would work out in his favor, for he could still tend to Ciderville and drive the school bus. He found the couple to be good Christians, who didn't allow drinking and smoking on the job, and he traveled with them eight years: "They were the greatest people I ever worked with. We never had a cross word."

All this time, Buster kept noting, "We're going to hire you," but never in all those years did he ever say "You've got the job!" Mostly they traveled in a 1955 Cadillac limousine all over Ohio, Virginia, Kentucky, West Virginia, Tennessee and the Carolinas. Sponsors for their big shows included Jim Walter Homes and Aunt Jemima Syrup.

Maybelle Carter traveled a lot in their troupe, and Buster would only let her or David do the driving. Among their stops were the Cherokee Theater in North Carolina, the Smoky Mountain Jubilee, Jim Walter Jubilee, Renfro Valley Barn Dance, half-time for University of Tennessee football games, the Pigeon Forge Coliseum, and drive-in theaters in both Harlan and Hazard, Kentucky, where listeners "applauded" by honking horns. Sometimes Scotty Stoneman, Mel Street or L. E. White worked shows with them.

During one session, L. E. White, who had written numerous songs for Conway Twitty (among them "To See My Angel Cry"), was asked a favor by Mel Street, who said, "I think I've written a pretty good song called 'Borrowed Angel,' can you get it to Conway for me?" Well, L. E. took it to Twitty, who turned it down. But White told Street, "That's a hit song, so go cut it yourself." Mel did just that and the rest is history, it became his first Top Ten in 1972, followed by such classics as "Lovin' On Back Streets" and "I Met A Friend Of Your's Today."

Once L. E. told David, "Let's do something to make money. We could produce records for wannabe singers, using Conway's studio (since he had access to it after six p.m.). We would produce records and have a thousand pressed for them. We would charge the artists a fee for production, which would include our fee, the studio (time) and musicians. What the artists do with their records is up to them - mail to DJ's, sell them on shows or give them away."

David had the personality to talk to people. He would spot a girl at a show who wanted to sing professionally, go up to her, saying, "How'd you like to go to Nashville and cut a record?" Of course, she would be thrilled and David would take her to Nashville where he and L. E. produced a record on her. The duo did a lot of these sessions, earning a fair sum of money, until they grew tired of this venture.

In 1968, West met Joe Morrell, who owned music stores in New Johnsonville and Bristol. He was doing quite well selling instruments at his stores, and let David put a few of his instruments for sale at Ciderville. Before long, David was selling instruments like wild fire and got orders from all over.

By 1969, they were making more money in the music store than selling cider. Morrell tipped off David about Jobbers, where he could obtain Martin and Fender dealerships, and even vouched for him when they asked for credit references. When the Fender representative came to see West, they wrote up a one hundred and sixty thousand dollar order. David offered to pay part of that in advance, but the Fender agent said, "No. Wait until you sell them."

Bill Carson, designer of the Stratocaster Guitar, told David he had a great credit reference in Joe Morrell. Well, David never had a check bounce and his Ciderville Music Store had more string instruments on sale than anyone else in the area, including basses, banjos, guitars, fiddles, mandolins, among others. The cider business got pushed aside as the instrument sales escalated.

During this time, David met Luke Brandon, who dropped by the music store. After making Luke's acquaintance, they soon became friends forever. Luke had played guitar for such notables as Don Gibson, Cowboy Copas, The Everly Brothers and even pop star Trini Lopez. Luke was one of the finest players in Knoxville, Nashville or anywhere. And Luke made all the musicians around him sound better. But Luke did what he wanted to do, when he wanted, and never stayed rooted to any one place. David admitted, "I owe Luke for my hot licks and chords." But he added, "Luke Brandon was a funny guy," before commencing a story he recalled about him: "Once he was up North and they gave him a pony for his kid back in Rockwood. Luke put the pony in his trailer. When they got to Rockwood, the pony ran away and Luke ran up and down all the streets in Rockwood, trying to catch that pony. Finally he caught him and got him home to his kids. They named him Rosebud."

In 1974, David quit playing for Bonnie Lou & Buster. Their work had slacked off, and he felt his own businesses needed his full attention. But then colorful Jake Butcher appeared on the scene, offering him so much money, he couldn't say no. He also was aware that Cas Walker supported Butcher, a banker and leading political figure in the 1970s and '80s. They played everywhere that Butcher campaigned, from 1974-'78, covering ninety-five counties. West felt Butcher was a scholar and gentleman (though controversial).

When playing the Cherokee Country Club, Butcher was dressed in tuxedo, like the other banquet guests, while David's band wore overalls, red ties and plaid shirts When they arrived, Butcher told those in charge, "This is my band. I want them to have a steak dinner just like the rest of us." David remembered that Jake liked to hear the songs "Down In Union County" and "Foggy Mountain Breakdown."

David regarded Scotty Stoneman as one of the finest fiddlers he ever worked with. Scotty was the son of Ernest Stoneman and an occasional

The Stonemans: Scotty (from left), Pop, Van, Roni, Donna and Jimmy Stoneman.

member of the award-winning Stoneman Family band. Bob Bean, manager of the group and husband of Scotty's sister Donna, was with the act when they had their syndicated TV series (1966-'68) sponsored by Gingham Girl Flour. Scotty, however, had problems and only joined the group three or four times, but Bean agreed Scotty was a phenomenal musician. He was a five-time winner of National Fiddling Championships, and his group, Bluegrass Champs, also were victorious in the *Arthur Godfrey Talent Scouts* (1956) TV competition.

Once David had a neat, new girlfriend whom Cas Walker had introduced him to: Mary Madison. She drove a 1965 Chevrolet, and Scotty Stoneman often drove with the new twosome. But as time passed, as David pointed out, "Darned if Scotty didn't marry her!" Mary did her best to care for Scotty the rest of his life; however, he was a free spirit, and at the end was at Bob Bean's home when he died. The music world lost a fiddlin' wonder, when Scotty passed in March 1973, reportedly from alcohol poisoning. (He was forty years old.)

Singer Ava Barber was performing on the *Cas Walker Show*, prior to becoming a regular on the national Lawrence Welk telecast in California. Introducing her, the WROL announcer stated Ava was sweet sixteen and never been kissed. "I'll fix that," thought David, who grabbed her as she came off stage and kissed her, then told Ava, "Now they can say you're sweet sixteen and end it there."

Karen Luethke met David in 1973, as she used to visit Ciderville on Saturday nights. Soon she and he became close friends. Karen noted, "He made me think I was special. He makes everyone feel they are part of his life." According to Karen, David must have known forty-two women, but she became David's soul mate. Mostly, she and David were homebodies, spending their time at the Ciderville store and shows. Karen even sold tickets there, though occasionally they did venture to the night spot out on Clinton Highway where Don Gibson entertained.

Faye West smiled remembering when David was young, noting he was shy and bashful around girls, "But he really changed when he got older." Karen recalled the band that played with David at Ciderville, particularly fiddler Dailey Carson, who wanted to play, but really didn't play well. Yet, he was always there. One time in mid-winter, David was on the ground, working on his car, and there was Dailey just fiddlin' away.

Another fiddler, Garfield Hensley, who was good (when you kept the spirits away from him) sparked this recollection: "Once the banjo player was playing a banjo tune and Garfield's bow went right through the head of that banjo! Then there was a time they were playing in Crab Orchard, Tennessee, and Garfield was really getting down with a fiddle breakdown, and all of a sudden lost his bow. It went sailing over the stage!" Karen said the only original band member still with David at Ciderville is Rowdy Cope. While Karen and David have been through a lot, she insists: "We are still together, still the same soul mates we have always been."

Indeed it's a treat these days to tour Ciderville, just to see all the memorabilia. Pictures cover the walls in the Ciderville Show Room, the museum, a showplace for Knoxville musicians, in the instrument room, and even the restroom. It's guaranteed that if a musician ever played Knoxville, his picture is somewhere on the walls of Ciderville.

David West as a businessman was a success, and as a musician, he seems to have played everywhere. He always tried to improve on everything he did, whether it be producing records, running Ciderville, doing floor sanding, conducting a turkey shoot, selling produce and instruments in his stores, as well as popcorn from a truck, or operating an art shop, and even driving a school bus. Part of his success formula was surrounding himself with those who knew a lot.

"Instead of book learning, I got it from first-hand experience," he emphasized, boasting the words "I can't" were never heard in his business place. Even when some other musicians seemed jealous of him, David didn't take the bait. Having grown up with sisters who encouraged him and never displayed any jealousy, he learned you didn't have to be number one to succeed. He also believes wisdom, knowledge and facts aren't free, you pay for them with hard work and experience.

Sure, David has one regret. He wishes Knoxville would've appreciated country music as much as Nashville players did. Then maybe RCA could have built their studio there instead of Nashville. In hindsight, Knoxville had very talented artists that Nashville inherited, among them Roy Acuff, Chet Atkins, Archie Campbell, Bill Carlisle, Don Gibson and Carl Smith.

West is comforted somewhat remembering that even at the height of his popularity, Bill Carlisle loved performing at Ciderville. Of course,

Carlisle knew West many years and as long as health permitted played Ciderville at least once every year, usually performing with West's Cider Mountain Boys. After he grew older, Bill confided to David, "I only play two places now: Ciderville and the Opry." (Country Hall of Famer Carlisle died in 2003 at age 94.)

David enjoys old sayings such as: 1) "If you win an argument, what would you win? You're just spinning your wheels." - Bill Carlisle. 2) "The majority of good people will help you, if they see you're trying to help yourself." - David's dad. 3) "The love of making money is 'Like Faith Without Works' (Is Dead)." - James 2:14-26. 4) When David was asked, "What would you do if you were elected president of the U.S.?" His answer: "Kneel down and pray, 'Lord, I want you to forgive me for murder,' then I'd shoot myself."

It's true, David never strayed far from his father's teaching, "Don't forget your upbringing." West mused, "There are many stories to be told about the artists around Knoxville. Some are too bad to tell, but too good to keep to yourself. Some have been enlarged, but sometimes truth is not quite as exciting as legend."

Here's David West's Ciderville Apple Cider Recipe.

1. Get a big truck.
2. Load the truck with good, juicy Virginia apples.
3. Grind up apples in a Cider Mill.
4. Press juice from apple pulp.
5. Strain juice (save pulp for animal food).
6. Boil juice and pour into bottles for "sweet cider." (West bought his bottles from Pepsi Bottling. Bottles should be washed thoroughly with soap and water, then rinsed with vinegar.)
7. For "sharp cider," punch two or three holes in the lid and keep for three or four days.
8. For "hard cider," punch two or three holes in the lid and let ferment for ten days.

Note: A bushel of apples averages two-and-a-half gallons of sweet cider. West sold his cider for five cents a cup, sharp and hard cider for ten cents a cup.

David West Interview, April 2016.

David West

Listeners enjoy trio of pickers (forefront): Larry Demarcus, West and Robbie Evans.

5 DAVID FARMER ...
Clinch Valley Fiver

"I like mountain music
Good old mountain music
Played by a good Hillbilly Band . . ."

Frank Weldon/John Cavanaugh (Hoosier Hot Shots)

David Farmer is the ideal person to reminisce with, regarding David West. His whole life relates to the music we now call "country." As a child of five and six years old, he remembers listening to their battery-operated radio and hearing WSM's *Grand Ole Opry* all the way from Nashville; and that he and his mother rode the bus just to watch WNOX's *Mid-Day Merry-Go-Round* on a regular basis. It was a fifty-mile trip one way. His memory flips back to Carl Smith and even at Farmer's young age, he would try to remember the words he heard and the melodies. Riding home aboard the bus, he would stand on a seat and sing Carl Smith songs for the bus audience, as passengers delighted in the child's impromptu performances.

Naturally when David grew up, music became his life, too. He began his career, playing guitar for *The Jim Fagan Show* on WYSH-Clinton, Tennessee. That was also the first show he remembers David West playing on. Fagan had stopped by Ciderville, and after hearing West on banjo, asked him to play on his show. West, just a beginner, didn't yet have his own band. As it became time for Fagan to introduce West that first night on the show, he said, "We're now going to hear a banjo tune from my guest, David West. Take it away, David!" But West didn't appear, as he was still off stage, tuning his banjo. There was nothing but silence, dead air time, which is just about as bad as it gets in broadcasting. Again Jim called out, "Take it away, David!" West suddenly appeared on stage, but hadn't yet finished tuning, meaning for his radio debut, he played an out-of-tune banjo.

When David got home, he asked his sisters, "How did I do?" They said, "O.K., but it took so long for you to play, after you were introduced. We thought the radio had gone dead." West acknowledged that taught him a lesson, to never allow any dead space while broadcasting. Say something. Even back then, David West listened and learned.

David Farmer and his guitar, 1969.

Farmer said, "In all the years I've known David West, he was never at a loss for something to do. I had an aunt that taught him at Claxton Elementary School. She knew that David and I were friends and in later years, we had several conversations about David. She said that David didn't pay much attention in school: "It wasn't that he couldn't do the work, he just had no interest. He would sit and look out the window. He was always preoccupied. I actually wrote on his report card that David does not pay attention." After my aunt died, in later years, David bought her old home place. She misjudged David. She didn't think he would do well. He just cared less about education. If it had nothing to do with music or making money, he just wasn't interested. In all the years I've known David, he always did something, whether it was driving a school bus, sanding floors or building Ciderville. He did everything he could to earn money."

Pam Tillis and David Farmer (2010).

While David was driving a school bus, John Rice Irwin was Superintendent of Tennessee's Anderson County School System. Even though they became friends, they didn't know that each of them liked to play music. When they discovered the other played instruments, they became fast friends. As things turned out, West also became a great musician. He didn't start out as a banjo player, he started out on a harmonica. That didn't work out too well. Then he began playing guitar, but when he heard the banjo, it just clicked with him. His first banjo was a cheap one and difficult to play. The strings were too high off the neck, a usual thing with cheap instruments. Then he got a Gibson and mastered the instrument.

Back in those days, a lot of businesses started up around Ciderville. People were attracted to the music and musicians they heard there. Some of those people were talented, too. David started his music store and people gathered around to hear the bluegrass music the pickers were playing there. So, West expanded and built his *Music Barn*. It was small then, no dance floor, just a place to come and hear a band and sit in the chairs provided. What had started out as a place to sell cider, he enlarged and kept building, until he had what we know now as Ciderville. Rowdy Cope was an original member of David's band when he built the music barn, and is still with him today. Farmer took over the radio show in the late 1960s and called it David Farmer and The Clinch Valley Five. It used that name for years. Farmer did commercials for Harvest Bread, Fox Motor Company and Lak Jewelry.

David West and David Farmer became close friends. When Hubert Waggoner, a booker, heard West and Farmer play, he started booking them on weekends. Then they got with a bigger booker, Lefty Combs, out of Mt. Vernon, Kentucky. Lefty wanted to put a bluegrass group on the road, so West and Farmer signed with Combs at the same time. Lefty scheduled the bookings, so that they each worked every other weekend. One weekend Farmer took care of Ciderville, and the next weekend West took care of Ciderville.

Both had good bands. West's band was called The Cider Mountain Boys. Lefty booked sixty or seventy theaters, and his shows were well planned, usually consisting of a matinee music show, then a Western movie, and after the screening, there was music again from 7:30-8:30 p.m.

They also played clubs or "road houses." Back then there wasn't much difference in those road houses from the way they were in the 1940s. The musicians called them "skull orchards." Some even had chicken-wire stretched across the stage to stop the bottles that might be thrown, to protect the musicians. Unruly patrons threw bottles for different reasons, some for the fun of it, or if they didn't dig the music, and maybe they were just too drunk to know better. But mostly those were fun days, and the musicians were all close and usually got along with one another.

David Farmer, like West, did other things besides play music. For instance, he became an apprentice watchmaker, working for Gene Dagley, who just happened to be a great rhythm guitar player. In the late '60s, John Hitch became manager of the new *Tennessee Valley Barn Dance* at WNOX. Farmer played a lot of shows for him, including *The Renfro Valley Barn Dance*. Sidney Spiva, a steel guitarist, was also on a lot of the shows with Farmer. Spiva later backed Dolly Parton. Farmer worked a lot with Nashville artists himself, while being booked by Hitch, among them were Bobby G. Rice, Wayne Kemp, Bill Phillips, Johnny Rodriguez and Archie Campbell.

Farmer moved to Tallahassee, Florida, for awhile and regularly played at showrooms in the Holiday Inn, The Hilton Hotel and Ramada Inn. In Panama City, he worked at The Golden Spoke. When Farmer moved back to Tennessee, he worked with an ambulance service as a Paramedic. Then he got back in with David West and Luke Brandon, working at places like The Museum of Appalachia and Stage Four.

Farmer said, "David West was a fantastic banjo player. He was asked a lot of times why he didn't go to Nashville. West knew if he went there, he would be traveling all the time for union scale, then about two dollars a day. He knew what he wanted to do and stayed home, and remained in better financial shape. I personally feel that West was as good or better than any banjo player in Nashville."

David Farmer, on the other hand, resumed working out of Nashville. For instance in 1973, Farmer met legendary Lefty Frizzell at George Jones' Possum Hollow Club. Soon he was doing shows with Lefty for about a year-

and-a-half. Farmer recalled, "By then, Lefty, bless his heart, was trying for a come back. He died in July 1975."

As Farmer noted, "David West and I traveled in an old Cadillac limousine and at one time we traveled in a bus. The Cadillac and the bus had Ciderville and hillbilly cartoon people painted on the sides. People used to gather around taking pictures." According to Farmer, West is a down-to-earth person, who doesn't put on airs: "He is a master at playing banjo, but somehow not a polished entertainer. He is more like Hank Williams, that is, when he walks on stage, he has the audience in his hand. They relate to him. He comes off as completely off the woodwork, homespun with a lot of 'hillbilly talk.' The people just believe in him." Farmer added that he never saw West take a drink or smoke.

Jodie Harbin, David West and David Farmer play at Knoxville Historic Center.

"He liked the females, but was never married," Farmer continued. "However, he's had multitudes of girlfriends. Ciderville became a great showcase. David would put anybody on stage. Nothing throws him and his energy level has always been high."

For the past seven years, David Farmer has been a part of Ciderville. West leaves the show up to Farmer, his friend, James Perry and Danny Farmer. They are in charge of the Saturday night shows, which means getting the musicians and artists off and on the show on time, while keeping the audience happy. In between times, they run a country music radio show, playing all the yesteryear music so loved back then, and also providing interesting chatter, regarding the records and artists. For them, it's a labor of love and great fun for fans, who like hearing that good old country music, played by a good hillbilly band. (Interview with David Farmer, in Nashville, Tennessee, April 2016.)

Members of the W.N.O.X.
"Mid-Day Merry-Go-' Round"
1938-1963

Lowell Blanchard – A.P. & "Mother Maybelle" Carter – Archie   Campbell
June, Helen & Anita Carter – Molly O'Day & Lynn Davis – J   Carson
Jerry Collins – Harry Nides – Bill Lawson – Hubert Car   Durham
Tony Musco – Charlie Hagaman – Cliff Steer + Larry Downing   Buck "Houchins
Troy Hatcher + Ray Myers – "Rabbit" Edmonds – Chet Atkins
"Buck" Fulton ("Huckleberry") – "Red" Rector – Fred Smith + Carl Story
Claude Boone – "SouthPaw" Thacker – "Hack" & Clyde Johnson – Homer Harris
"Kitty" Wells – Johnny Wright + Jack Anglin ("Johnny & Jack") – "Cowboy" Copas
"Shorty" Sharp + "Natchez the Indian" – Elton Britt – Jim Ed Thomas
"Pappy" Cheshire & "The Ozark Mountaineers" – Bill Norman
The Louvin Brothers + "Monk & Sam" + "Curly" & Johnny Shelton
"Sunshine Slim" Sweet ‡ Roy Lanham + Lonnie Glosson
Wally Fowler & "The Oak Ridge Quartet" + "Curly" Kinsey
"Mom & Pop" Loden & "Sonny" James – Arthur "Q". Smith (Jas Pritchett)
Tommy Covington – "Pee Wee" King + Zeke & Wiley Morris
Cliff & Bill Carlisle & "Sonny Boy Tommy" – "Hot Shot Elmer"
Frankie Turner – John Gallagher + Clayton McMitchen
Abner Simms – Charlie Monroe – "Smiling" Eddie Hill
"Homer & Jethro" – Aytchie Burns – Junior Huskey
Bill & Joe Burchfield – Jake Tullock + "Little Robert" – Jimmy Murphy
Billy Bowman – Leonard Dabney – "Honey" Wilds – "Salty" Holmes – Max Terhune
Kirk McGee – Shannon Grayson + Marion Taylor – Charlie Elza ("KY Slim")
Paul Warren + "Smoky" White (John Whiting) – "Red" Kirk
"Bonnie Lou & Buster" + Tommy Trent – "Lost John" Miller
Don Gibson + "Speedy" Krise + Randolph Family
Charlie Pickle – Gene McGee + "Bud & Jeter" – Hoke Jenkins
"Tex" Isley – "Bud" Osborne + Mac Wiseman – L.E. White
Jack Green – Carl Smith – Burk Barbour – "Cotton" Galyon
"Buddy" Baines + Luke Brandon + Roy Sneed
"PAPPY" GUBE BEAVER

*This plaque denotes numerous cast players at the WNOX
Mid-Day Merry-Go-Round (1938-1963). Note that the camera
flash nearly obscured the upper right corner names Archie
(Grandpappy) Campbell, James & Martha Carson and Dave
Durham, but they were indeed entertainers on this historic
radio program.*

PART TWO

THE ARTISTS . . .

Prospero II: *"We are such stuff, as dreams are made on . . ."*
The Tempest, Act 4, Scene 1 – William Shakespeare

6 THE MUSIC MAKERS ...

The history of *The Mid-Day Merry-Go-Round* and *The Tennessee Barn Dance*, like all history, is not simply what has happened, it is the way what happened is remembered. Any old-timer, when asked what he remembers about those days will always begin with, *"Well-I-I, I remember . . ."* and he will always come up with at least one good story.

Wanda White Matthews remembers playing *The Tennessee Barn Dance* starting in the '50s. She recalls that her group, consisting of Wanda, Carlton Scruggs, Jack White and Hairl Hensley, sang the final song on the *Barn Dance's* last show. This group sang mostly country songs, but on that special night, Lowell Blanchard asked them to sing a hymn to close the show. They sang Reverend J. K. Alwood's 1885 "The Unclouded Day."

"O they tell me of a home far beyond the skies / O they tell me of a home far away / O they tell me of a home where no storm clouds rise / O they tell me of an unclouded day. . . ."

Wanda also remembered meeting Patsy Cline backstage one night. Patsy was a guest on the *Barn Dance*. Lowell Blanchard had heard her on CBS-TV's *Arthur Godfrey's Talent Scouts* and asked her to sing on the *Barn Dance* for five hundred dollars. Patsy told Wanda she was leaving after the show to spend a weekend with her husband Charlie Dick in North Carolina.

Raise a glass to toast all those performers who sacrificed their comfortable fireside to play on the "Kerosene Circuit," schoolhouses with no electricity, church basements, grange halls and any place with a stage. There was no place to change clothes, except in the car, an alley or a makeshift dressing area. They took baths in mountain streams, and often ran out of gas and blew tires. When asked, "Why did you do it?," their answer was usually, "What else would I do?"

The following pages tell the story of many of the ones who were center stage at *The Mid-Day Merry-Go-Round* and *The Tennessee Barn Dance*, and then felt like they had to travel on.

> *"All the world's a stage*
> *And all the men and women merely players*
> *They have their exits and their entrances*
> *And each man in his day plays many parts."*
>
> Shakespeare

7 ROY ACUFF . . .

"In the pines, In the pines
Where the sun never shines
And I shiver when the cold winds blow . . ."

Jimmie Davis, Hoyt Bryant, Clayton McMichen

Roy Claxton Acuff was born September 15, 1903 in Maynardville, Union County, Tennessee, in a house within a stone's throw of the courthouse. When Roy finished grade school, his "Papa" borrowed Maynardville's only automobile, a 1917 Hupmobile, for a move to Fountain City, a suburb of Knoxville. They didn't have to move furniture, as nobody owned furniture. You simply rented a house with furniture. Papa had attended Carson-Newman College and was a lawyer and a Baptist preacher. Being an educated man, he wanted to move nearer Knoxville, because the schools were better.

As Roy grew up, he listened to the high, mountain singing of his neighbors and learned from his father how to play the fiddle. He attended church singings where he was taught out of shape-note hymnals. He also listened to Victrola Records by people like The Skillet Lickers, trying to play along, though Roy didn't aspire to be a musician. Within his circle of friends, people didn't get paid for singing or "sawing" a fiddle. They did these things for fun.

Actually, Roy wanted to be a star baseball player. In fact, Roy excelled in sports. In high school he earned thirteen letters, four each in football and basketball and five in baseball. Not bad, considering he only weighed one hundred and thirty pounds soaking wet.

Acuff played some semi-pro baseball. In 1929, scouts for the New York Yankees came through Knoxville, and invited Roy to their training camp. It seemed his dream had come true. But, that summer of '29, Roy went on a fishing trip to Soldier Key in Florida with a friend, Ross Smith. Roy, who grew up in the mountains, had never been exposed to sun like that in the Keys. He blistered so badly he couldn't sleep. A few days later, Roy was playing ball at home, and at the end of the fourth inning, passed out and was hospitalized. The doctor said he had suffered sunstroke, and Acuff's days as an athlete were over. Reportedly, he spent a year in bed.

While recuperating at home, he discovered The Carter Family and Jimmie Rodgers on the radio. Radio had come to Knoxville, when WNOX and WROL went on the air. Roy loved to hear the break-down fiddle, the guitar music of the hills and the gospel music of the church. He also listened to Vernon Dalhart, The Skillet Lickers, and Fiddlin' John Carson.

Eventually, Roy picked up his father's old fiddle and tried to pick out songs, playing by ear. That fiddle had been hand-carved by Al Cassidy of Maynardville in 1907. He spent hours each day sawing away on the old music from the hills. Suddenly he realized, thanks to radio and records, hillbilly music had become a business.

The Crazy Ten-E-Seeans: kneeling Roy Acuff and Red Burns,
standing (from left) Jess Easterday, Kentucky Slim,
(probably) Dynamite Hatcher and James Clell Summey.

In 1932, and almost thirty years old, Acuff played his first professional gig with a medicine show headed by Doc Hauer. Soon he became steeped in the folk music of East Tennessee. Finally, Roy discovered John Copeland's Garage. He found that in addition to being a mechanic and a fox hunter, Copeland was a pretty good country fiddler. They became good friends and Copeland would play his fiddle and tell Roy stories about songs he played like "Sally Goodin." Then Roy started taking his fiddle to the garage, where he and Copeland played and told stories by the hour. Word got around and soon others started coming by with their instruments.

As Roy played on his own front porch, his first stage, he had the feeling that he really wanted to be a performer. He played songs that he had heard on the radio or at Copeland's Garage. He played that fanciful front porch circuit for about a year.

"Doc" Stevens owned a corner drugstore in Knoxville and at this drugstore a lot of musicians hung out. Finally, Doc built an outdoor stage on a vacant lot next door. It became a sort of a homespun talent show, until one day a group called The Tennessee Crackerjacks came by to play. In the band were Jess Easterday, guitar; Bob Wright, mandolin; and Clell Summey, Dobro (later known as Cousin Jody). They had everything but a leader. Roy told them: "Boys, meet your new leader!"

That was the real start of Roy Acuff's career. He had done other type shows, the medicine show, the stage at Doc Stevens, talent shows and hoedowns, but this was the real thing.

David West said that his father, Claude West, and Sam Jones, a musician, told him that Roy once even managed a roadhouse called The Pink Palace, just a short distance from where Ciderville is now. Acuff entertained the people by walking around the tables and playing his fiddle for patrons.

The Crackerjacks bought an old REO sedan. Now the Crackerjacks were ready for the road. They also started hanging out at WROL. They pestered WROL, until finally, to get them off their backs, the station offered them a program, sponsored by Dr. Hamilton, Dentist. After a short time, Roy heard that Lowell Blanchard at WNOX was starting a new show called *The Mid-Day Merry-Go-Round.*

Soon afterwards, Blanchard offered the Crackerjacks a spot on *The Merry-Go-Round*, so they switched stations, and played to a full house every day. At that point, WNOX and *The Merry-Go-Round* was the nation's first local, continually-running country music station, and one of the more important radio shows in the history of music. It made Roy and the band a name in show business. Within months, the show became so popular they moved to the one-thousand, five-hundred-seat Market Hall. A nickel admission was charged. *The Merry-Go-Round* gave young musicians a tremendous opportunity, of course, because truly there weren't enough spots for musicians to go around.

Each member of the band was making fifty cents a show. Finally, Roy requested higher wages for his band, but was refused. So in 1935, they returned to WROL. Roy and his Tennessee Crackerjacks had stayed over at WNOX only eight months.

One day Allen Stout, an announcer at WROL, told the listening audience that the band was just a bunch of "Crazy Tennesseans," a name that stuck. They did noon shows, opened the station in the morning, and filled in at odd hours during the day and night, all this from a small studio. Roy said, "Looking back, when they did *The Merry-Go-Round*, it was pretty professional." That show was done in a big auditorium, in front of an audience. WROL, with a small studio, was a far cry from *The Mid-Day Merry-Go-Round* at WNOX.

Lead singers almost did not exist in those days, but with The Crazy Tennesseans, Roy filled that role. In the band were Red Jones, Dynamite Hatcher, Clell Summey, Jess Easterday and Tiny Sarrett. Sometimes Pete (Oswald) Kirby would join them (but he was not a regular, until after Roy went to the Opry). Road shows were the mainstays for early performers. When Roy got a date set, he would announce on the radio where they would be playing, places like Clinton, Sevierville or Dandridge. They split the proceeds with their sponsor, seventy per cent to the band, thirty per cent to the sponsor. Admissions were usually twenty-five cents for adults and ten cents for kids. They usually cleared five or six dollars each, and got back to the station just in time to do their morning show.

In 1935, Charlie Swain had a program at WROL with his band, The Black Shirts. Roy was listening when Swain sang a chorus of "The Great Speckled Bird," to the tune of "I'm Thinking Tonight Of My Blue Eyes."

This was Roy Acuff's home in Maynardville, Tenn.

Roy asked Charlie to write down the words for him. Charlie did and Roy paid him fifty cents for the lyrics. When Roy sang it on the air, he got more favorable mail about it, than for any song he had ever done.

On October 26, 1936, Roy went to Chicago and recorded "The Great Speckled Bird" for the American Record Company (ARC). William R. Callaway was the producer, and the backing band included Clell Summey, guitar; Red Jones, bass; Dynamite Hatcher, harmonica; and Jess Easterday, guitar. Besides " . . . Bird," they recorded twenty songs. Much later, Roy found out that The Reverend Guy Smith had written five or six verses to the song, based on the ninth verse of the twelfth chapter of Jeremiah in the Bible: *"What a beautiful thought I am thinking / Concerning a Great Speckled Bird / Remember her name is recorded / On the pages of God's Holy Word . . ."*

In 1936, when Roy recorded "The Great Speckled Bird," he knew six verses. Songs at that time were usually made up of five verses. That was what he recorded, but when he went back to Knoxville, he wrote four more verses. With the verse he didn't record on the first session, plus the four new verses he wrote, he recorded five more verses in 1937, calling it "The Great Speckled Bird, Number Two." In total, he had recorded thirty-four sides for the record company.

The Crazy Tennesseans became known by thousands of East Tennesseans, who listened to WNOX and WROL. Roy not only sang, but did the fiddling and his yo-yo tricks were popular even then at shows. They did "heart" songs, humorous songs, hoedowns and comedy skits. Roy could fill studios or auditoriums with lyrics like, *"Down to Union County, down to Union County, down to Union County, for to see my Suzie Ann . . ."*

36

Roy's unique country voice got him a Columbia Records contract, while still in Knoxville. Acuff and his band became popular over Knoxville radio, but his desire was to go to Nashville. He talked to Pee Wee King and his manager, Joe L. Frank, and they succeeded in getting Roy a guest spot on the *Grand Ole Opry* in 1937. The Opry's location then was the Dixie Tabernacle on Fatherland Street in East Nashville. It was a drafty barn-like structure with a sawdust floor. It was a cold and rainy winter night when the lonesome looking Smoky Mountain boy took the stage. He was so excited and nervous that he was considered good, but by no means great. After the show, everyone was "polite," Roy said, "David Stone, head of the Artists Bureau, said goodbye politely."

Roy went back to Knoxville and forgot all about the Opry. But, in two weeks the Opry sent him the mail he had received after his performance in two bushel baskets. This had not impressed the WSM bosses, and Judge George D. Hay didn't think much of Acuff's singing or fiddling. Announcer David Cobb even told the Opry manager that the sooner Roy Acuff found another way to make a living, the better it would be for him. David Stone, however, was so impressed with the amount of mail received, that he offered Roy another chance to audition on February 5, 1938. On February 10, he got a letter from Stone offering him a spot on the Opry, plus a series of seven a.m. programs.

Oddly enough, Roy was skittish about leaving Knoxville, having already been turned down once by the Opry; however, Joe L. Frank encouraged him to go. Roy guested on Pee Wee King's *Royal Crown Show* and got a standing ovation. This time they invited Roy and his Crazy Tennesseans to stay.

All the modern day books cite their name as "Crazy Tennesseans," however, on the side of their traveling trailer it's written as the CRAZY TEN-E-SEEANS. (See picture.) Yet WSM wasn't very impressed by the band's name.

Roy moved to Nashville, into a trailer in suburban Madison. As a WSM cast member, his first appearance occurred on February 19, 1938. While the name Crazy Tennesseans ushered him into the Opry, Harry Stone felt the name a little disrespectful to the state of Tennessee. Since Roy knew the WSM signal was going all the way out to Clinch Mountain and maybe beyond, he agreed to a name change. Roy knew about a band in Knoxville, headed by Esco Hankins, calling themselves The Smoky Mountain Boys. He liked that name and ran it by Stone, who liked it. Thus, Roy went to meet with Hankins and the two decided to exchange names, meaning Esco and his boys were suddenly Crazy Tennesseans.

The new Smoky Mountain Boys boasted Acuff as lead vocalist and fiddler; Easterday on guitar and mandolin; Jones on guitar; Summey on Dobro; and Tiny Sarrett, their female backing singer. In 1939, however, Jones, Summey and Sarrett left the band to return to Knoxville. Acuff hired Oswald Kirby, Dobro; Lonnie (Pap) Wilson, guitar; Jack Tindell, bass (all from Knoxville), and later hired farm girl Rachel Veach, singer-banjoist.

Knoxville's loss, as the saying goes, was Nashville's gain. While at the Opry, Roy was acclaimed "King of Country Music," and he remained on the show until his passing. Roy's familiar signature song "Wabash Cannonball" became his calling card. Acuff's penetrating Appalachian wail and sounds of ancient British balladry were silenced on November 23, 1992, and at his request he was buried seven-and-a-half hour after his death. He was eighty-nine years old. Then Opry manager Jerry Strobel said Roy had told him, "I want to be buried before people know I'm dead." The only people present at his graveside service were family members and his Smoky Mountain Boys. So ended the story of a boy, a fiddle and a dream.

"Who's gonna fill their shoes
Who's gonna play the Opry
And the 'Wabash Cannonball'
. . . Lord, I wonder who's gonna fill their shoes?"

Max D. Barnes-Troy Seals.

8 CHET ATKINS ...
Certified Guitar Player

Chester Burton Atkins was born June 20, 1924, near Luttrell, Tennessee. His father was a music teacher, piano-tuner, fiddle player and singer. They lived on Chet's grandfather's farm. He had a half-brother Jim who he idolized. Jim was thirteen years his senior, and later was part of The Les Paul Trio. His other siblings were Lowell, Nione and Willard.

Born into a troubled lot, Chet saw his parents, who were dirt poor, split up when he was six. Chet, who suffered from asthma, was also tongue-tied and shy. As a result of all this, he grew up lonely and scared.

As a youth, Chet heard his first country music over radio station WNOX-Knoxville. Both older brothers, Jim and Lowell, played music. At age six, Chet got a ukulele. If he broke a string, he had to pull a wire off the screen door to replace it. When he was nine, his stepfather traded a Model T Ford for fifteen dollars and an old Silvertone guitar. By the end of the year, an enthused Chet knew most of the major and minor first position chords.

A friend had a fiddle. A fiddle was the backbone of hoedowns and barn dances, the most popular instrument in their part of the hills. Naturally, Chet got hooked on the fiddle. Chet played every Saturday night for friends, who came to their house to dance and sing.

Atkins' first real public appearance was at school. He and Lowell were asked to play there for two hundred students. Still shy, Chet was a nervous wreck, but somehow the boys got through "The Wildwood Flower." When he was eleven, Chet's health failed. Diagnosed with a bad case of asthma, the doctor said a change of climate might help Chet, so he went to live with Dad in Columbus, Georgia.

In Georgia, Chet could see snake tracks in the dusty roads. At night, he listened to music on the radio from Knoxville and Atlanta. While living in Georgia, he began to experiment pickin' guitar with his fingers. He learned to play "Leavin' On That New River Train" and "Trouble In Mind." By Fall 1937, Chester's health had improved and he returned home to Mom in Luttrell.

Learning WNOX sponsored an amateur contest on a Saturday night, open to all, Chet and Lowell went down to the Strand Theater tryouts. Its marquee proclaimed: "WNOX Amateur Show, Tonight At 7." The brothers competed, playing "Foggy Mountain Top," then Chet did a chorus of "Cacklin' Hen" on his fiddle, but their combined efforts only earned third prize.

Unfortunately, that Knoxville venture was one of Chet's last happy times in East Tennessee, because his health failed again. That meant Chet had to go back to Georgia to live with Dad, and only returned to Luttrell for short visits afterwards.

A lot of stations in the South were playing more country music. Chet was an early admirer of Les Paul, with whom brother Jim and bassist Ernie Newton, formed The Les Paul Trio, heard on WLS-Chicago. Chet found himself influenced by Les's playing. Then one night he tuned in Merle Travis, and found the clever way Travis played melody and rhythm at the same time was closer to Chet's evolving style of pickin'.

Chet listened intently to the radio, trying to imitate guitar licks he heard. Once he mastered the pro's playing, he added the licks to his collection. When Dad landed a job in Cincinnati, Chet went back to Luttrell, where he assembled a two-tube radio and began listening to the WNOX *Mid-Day Merry-Go-Round*. Tuning in daily, he longed to be on that show so bad he could taste it.

A friend told him about a songwriter in Knoxville. Chet decided to go and meet with this writer. When he got there, he met Mel Foree and Tommy Covington of WNOX. Mel Foree was impressed with Chet's musical ability and suggested, "Chester, I can get you a job at the station, if you're interested." An excited Atkins returned home to Luttrell and three days later, a friend of Foree's dropped by, telling him, "Mel Foree asked me to stop by and tell you they had a job for you over at the radio station, if you want it, playing fiddle." Five minutes later, Chet was on a bus to Knoxville to appear at WNOX.

The man at the desk told Chet he was supposed to see Archie Campbell and Bill Carlisle. "They need a fiddle player for their show," he explained. Chet found Archie and Bill with Lowell Blanchard. Archie noted, "Lowell Blanchard is the boss here." Chet replied, "My name is . . ." and suddenly tongue-tied, couldn't get his name across, prompting Archie to crack, "Maybe it's written on your fiddle," and they all burst into laughter.

Then the nervous fiddler blurted out his name, "It's Chester Atkins, I'm Jim Atkins' brother!" Lowell said, "Well, why didn't you say so in the first place. Let's see if it runs in the family." So Chet played "Sally Goodin," and was hired on the spot. His salary was three dollars a day, and he was on the air forty minutes later. His show business career was launched.

By 1942, Chet was eighteen and a veteran of nearly one year on the radio. He was playing fiddle with Archie and Bill. Both Archie and Bill played guitar, so they didn't need another guitarist. One night, coming home from a show date, Chet picked up Bill's Martin guitar and played a song as they rode along. It knocked Lowell Blanchard out. Blanchard said, "Why didn't you tell me you could play guitar like that! How would you like to be featured on *The Merry-Go-Round?*"

Chet merely smiled. When he appeared on *The Merry-Go-Round* the next day, he played "Seeing Nellie Home," "Bye, Bye Blues" and "Maggie." From that point on, Blanchard took a great interest in musician Chet Atkins. It was also in '42, Chet began working with the WNOX house band, The Dixieland Swingers, composed of Herbie Cooper, drums; Tommy Trent, guitar and vocals; and Tony Cianciola, accordion. Chet and the band became great friends, not only playing together, but also chasing girls together.

When Archie Campbell was called into the Navy, Bill and Chet were out of a job. Chet was depressed. Then he ran into Blanchard on the street. He asked Chet, "Where've you been? The staff band guitar player has been drafted. We need you." For the first month, Blanchard paid Atkins fifteen dollars weekly, then raised it to thirty dollars a week

It was now 1943 and everything at WNOX was live. They did more than one hundred and fifty half-hour programs weekly. Johnnie & Jack had a morning show at 6, until Jack Anglin was drafted. Johnnie Wright then teamed up with Eddie Hill, and Chet was hired to play fiddle for their troupe.

According to Johnnie, "In Fact, Chet was a better fiddler than he was a guitar picker." After that morning show, came Chet's appearance on *The Mid-Day Merry-Go-Round*. After that he usually took off for a personal appearance with Johnnie and Eddie, meaning Chet had his own private *Merry-Go-Round,* of sorts. They played everywhere, schoolhouses, theaters, even court houses. They loaded the three of them, plus Johnnie's singer-wife Kitty Wells, into Johnnie's 1937 Chevy sedan. Then tried finding room for the instruments.

One night they ran into a fierce rainstorm that flooded the engine. They got out to try and dry it out, but nothing worked. Somebody suggested pouring gas on it, then lighting it to dry it out. When they did that, it caught the gas in the carburetor on fire. Eddie Hill placed his new Stetson hat over the carburetor and put out the fire.

They had a p.a. (public address) system that worked off a car battery, since most of the venues they worked didn't have electricity. So they would arrive at a date, unpack, take the battery out of the car and perform. They also used this p.a. system when driving into town to advertise their show: *"Tonight in person at the grade school, the Johnnie Wright Show with Kitty Wells, Eddie Hill and Chester Atkins. See your favorite performers from Radio Station WNOX in Knoxville!"* They worked every night but Saturdays, for that's when they played *The Tennessee Barn Dance* at the Lyric Theater on Gay Street.

After three years at the station, Chet felt it was time to move on. It was a difficult decision to make for Chet felt WNOX was home. But Lowell Blanchard assured him he always had a home there. Chet decided to make a move to WLW-Cincinnati, and Blanchard saw him off at the station, saying, "Come right on back, if it isn't right for you."

As Chet rode along on the bus to Cincinnati, he changed his mind and decided to talk to John Lair at Renfro Valley. Lair had said he could use him, offering to pay him fifty dollars a week. This gave Chet the boost in ego he needed. But, he turned that job down and instead went on to see Mr. Chamberlain at WLW. Chamberlain hired him to start on the morning show the next day, and on *The Boone County Jamboree,* which evolved into *The Midwestern Hayride*. Louis (Louie) Innis was a band member at WLW and they became good friends. Chet also met his future wife, Leona Johnson, who worked at WLW. Homer & Jethro and The Delmore Brothers were there, and Merle Travis, Chet's idol, guested there.

On Christmas Eve 1945, however, the station cut back on staff musicians, so Chet and Louie were let go. But Atkins got in touch with Johnnie Wright at WPTF-Raleigh and he hired Chet but couldn't use Innis. When brother-in-law Jack Anglin was discharged from the Army, he rejoined Johnnie, who had to let Chet go. Atkins heard Red Foley was going to take over Roy Acuff's number one Opry spot, *The Prince Albert Show*, so he left for Chicago to see Foley. At that time, Foley was on the WLS-*National Barn Dance*. Chet initially went to Red's booker, Bill Ellsworth, and luckily, Red was in his office. Red said, "Play something for me, Chester." Chet did and Red then said the magic words, "Would you like to go to Nashville with me?" Chet enthusiastically responded, "Yes, Sir, I would!" Incidentally, Louie Innis, rhythm guitar player and comic, also went to Nashville with them.

The big thrill for Chet came that first night on *The Grand Ole Opry*, when Red Foley announced, "And now folks, Chester Atkins will play 'Maggie' on the acoustic guitar." That first night at the Opry seemed in retrospect, a mass of confusion to Chet. Not many mistakes happened in all that confusion, but at one point they announced Lew Childre. Childre didn't show, for he was across the alley at "Mom's" having a beer. When he came back later, the announcer stated, "Okay folks, Lew Childre has the string on his guitar fixed, and he will now play for you."

Six months later, word came down from the ad agency that Chet was no longer needed for the spot he was doing. Foley tried to talk him into staying, minus his featured spot, but Chet didn't want to be a sideman, so he quit.

Chet landed at KWTO in Springfield, Missouri, with Slim Wilson and The Tall Timbers Trio. Within a few weeks, he was given a show of his own. Si Simon was the booking agent for the show and he was the first person there to take an interest in Chet. Si put him on his Mutual Network Show *Corn's A' Crackin'*. It was almost as good a feeling as he had at WNOX, until he got fired by the man who took Simon's place.

Atkins called Lowell Blanchard, who hired him back at WNOX. Homer & Jethro were then working at WNOX. They put a show together, calling it *Chet Atkins and The Colorado Mountain Boys, Featuring Homer & Jethro*. People in East Tennessee, however, didn't seem to cotton to their music. Bluegrass was becoming popular, and they tried everything to make the act go. They even added an amateur act, and the winner appeared with them on *The Tennessee Barn Dance*.

A group came to WNOX from Poor Valley, Virginia, calling themselves The Carter Sisters and Mother Maybelle. Maybelle, a member of the Original Carter Family, was accompanied by daughters Anita, June and Helen. They were an instant success on both the *Barn Dance* and *Merry-Go-Round*. Ezra J. Carter, Maybelle's husband, managed the group and said to Chet, "We've been thinking we need another instrument in the group. You sound good, and we would like to have you join us. We'll cut you in for one-sixth of what we make."

Bingo! Chet went to work for The Carters. They traveled to dates in a new Frazier car. One night they had a flat tire in the rain. Chet, a true Southern gentleman, got out to change the tire. As the passing cars splashed water on him, however, he taught the girls how to cuss. They giggled every time he said a bad word.

They got a call to go to KWTO-Springfield, and Homer & Jethro had preceded them there. Springfield was beautiful and the girls and Chet were well received. Si Simon, once again Chet's boss, decided to syndicate their show, calling it *The Carter Family & Chet Atkins*. Simon told Chet, "You're getting too damn good. One of these days we're gonna lose you."

One day, singer George Morgan was at the station to do some transcriptions for Martha White Flour. While there, he heard the Carters and Chet. When he went home, he told the Martha White Agency how great their act was. Shortly after, an agent at Martha White called and wanted them to go to Nashville and audition for a spot on the Opry. Chet was trying to decide what to do and he called Fred Rose. Rose advised Chet, "Come on to Nashville. I can use you on recording sessions."

When Chet went to Nashville with his wife and daughter, he asked Don Davis, a steel guitar player, to find him an apartment. Don found them an upstairs apartment on Granada Avenue in East Nashville. Chet said, "It was ideal, if we had wanted to live in a sauna. There was no air conditioning, it was an attic with no insulation. And it was June!" They spent a lot of time that summer in nearby Shelby Park. Chet and The Carters were successful at the Opry. Then June and Anita got married and soon the girls broke up their act. Chet left the Opry to freelance as a musician.

Meanwhile, RCA's Steve Sholes started shuttling to Nashville from New York, to record his Southern acts. Sholes was probably the first record producer (after Decca's Paul Cohen) to see the potential of Nashville, as a recording center. From 1945 until 1957, Sholes handled all the country music for Victor.

In 1947, Sholes signed Chet Atkins to RCA. He had heard "Canned Heat," a transcription by Atkins, and was impressed by his guitar playing. Before long, Sholes started turning to Atkins to book the musicians on his recording sessions. Atkins and Sholes had long talks about the business of recording, and how it was growing in Nashville.

Chet said, "The basic guitar style I play was started by a black guy, Jim Mason, in Kentucky, who played a 'choke' style of guitar. He taught it to Mose Rager and to Ike Everly. Merle Travis learned his guitar style from Rager. Travis, in turn influenced me. However, later I was also influenced by Les Paul and Django Reinhardt."

In the early days of recording, it was still uncomplicated. Chet became deeply involved with recording, and one day Sholes said, "Chet, how would you like to take over the new RCA Studios we're building? You know the business and the people and the singers." Chet accepted, although he didn't know a thing about being an A&R (artists and repertoire) man. He learned and learned well. Chet gave a lot of credit to the good musicians in Nashville. He said, "It's the only thing that makes my job easier."

As time passed, Chet began to make country music more up-to-date. He started using symphony strings instead of steel guitar and fiddle, especially with artists like Eddy Arnold and songs like "Make The World Go Away." One musician said, "Chet Atkins saved country music. He made it respectable." (One wonders if Chet was taking Luke Brandon's ideas when he added strings.)

In 1973, Chet Atkins became one of the youngest members inducted into The Country Music Hall of Fame at age forty-nine. He was honored with a Lifetime Achievement Grammy in 1993.

Chet Atkins was never again to be a regular part of *The Mid-Day Merry-Go Round* or *The Grand Ole Opry,* but he never forgot the old days. Once when he played a show in Knoxville for a twenty-two thousand dollar fee, he told his audience that he still remembered the nights he slept on the couch in the WNOX studios. Chet Atkins died June 30, 2001 at age seventy-seven. As one DJ was heard saying, that was the night the *Nashville Sound* died.

Chet Atkins

44

9 THE BUTLERS: CARL AND PEARL . . .

"Don't let me cross over, stay out of my way
Cause you know that I love you, and I'm not the stealin' kind
But I'm faced with heartache, here at love's cheating line."

Penny Jay

Carl Robert Butler was born June 2, 1927 in Knoxville, Tennessee. He was playing guitar and singing by the age of twelve, and by the time he left high school was writing songs and playing in local clubs. Carl grew up influenced by Roy Acuff from neighboring Maynardville, and the old-time music he heard coming out of the hills.

From 1944 to 1946, Carl served in the military in Europe and North Africa. After his discharge, he formed The Lonesome Pine Boys. During the late '40s, Butler was being featured on WNOX's *Mid-Day Merry- Go-Round*. By the early 1950s, he was also appearing regularly on Knoxville television. His hanky-tonk style music helped established him as a solo artist.

Carl's song, "If Teardrops Were Pennies" became a classic Top Ten country single for Carl Smith, another Maynardville native, in 1951 (and a Top Five for Dolly and Porter in 1973). In 1952, Carl married sweet-voiced Pearl Dee Jones, born September 20, 1930 in Nashville. He was really beginning his professional career at that time. Carl called Pearl "Pearlie Mae" and said she was the best cook in town. Howard White, steel-guitarist, remembered Pearl when she was a waitress at a cafe across the street from WNOX.

Butler's own first country hit came in 1961, "Honky Tonkitis," a Top Twenty written by Tex Atchison. In 1962, he had the perfect song to bring Pearlie Mae in for a duet: "Don't Let Me Cross Over" (credited to Penny Jay, but insiders felt it was written by Arthur Q. Smith). She had previously only sung with Carl at family get-togethers. Their vocal teaming proved very successful, as "Don't Let Me Cross Over" stayed number one eleven weeks of its twenty-four week chart run for Columbia.

Their sound was not technically harmony singing, since Carl's vocals were always dominant. Pearl merely sang in the background, never taking solos; however, their sound caught on with listeners. That same year, Carl and Pearl Butler were invited to join WSM's *Grand Ole Opry*, exposure that broadened their song's success, as it crossed over into *Billboard's* Hot One Hundred pop chart, as well.

In 1964, they attained another Top Ten single, "Too Late To Try Again," written by Carl. Although the Butlers continued to record in the 1970s, they essentially retired to their ranch, Crossover Acres, near Franklin, Tennessee. Carl and Pearl Butler were the first successful male-female duet of the 1960's, setting standards for the likes of Porter and Dolly. They made guest appearances on the Opry until Pearl died at age sixty on March 1, 1988. Carl died September 4, 1992, age sixty-five.

Carl & Pearl Butler

10 ARCHIE CAMPBELL...
'Grandpappy'

Archie Campbell was born November 7, 1914 to James Thomas and Leona Campbell in Bulls Gap, Hawkins County, Tennessee. After graduating from Mars Hill College in Mars Hill, North Carolina, where he studied art, Archie started performing at WNOX-Knoxville.

Archie was a funny, talented man, and exactly what Lowell Blanchard needed on *The Mid-Day Merry-Go-Round*. Archie got started with Roy Acuff and The Crazy Tennesseans in 1936, and for a time performed as a comic character he dubbed "Grandpappy," which added life to the group.

Campbell also did a commercial segment on the *Merry-Go-Round* with Pee Wee King, sponsored by the Red Ash Charcoal Company (selling Red Ash Coal): Archie's lines were "Get your Red Ash Coals, get 'em while they're hot," but Archie, always the comic, would hesitate and stumble before he said "ash," suggesting he might be about to say "ass." Archie would say, "Get your Red-ah, uh, uh, ah, Ash Coal." Archie knew exactly what listeners would imagine. If he had actually said "ass" on the air, he would've been kicked off the air for good.

When Cliff Carlisle left the *Merry-Go-Round* to retire, Archie teamed with his brother Bill Carlisle. They later added Chet Atkins as a fiddle player. Archie and Bill did some comedy wrestling together on the show, and Archie did his Grandpappy act, while Bill did his "Hot Shot Elmer" routine. Their road shows usually sold out, as people wanted to see the performers they listened to every day on radio. There wasn't any television yet, so these radio characters existed mainly in their imagination. One lady thought Archie looked like Winston Churchill, in her mind, until she saw him.

The local groups that sponsored their venues on the road got twenty-five per cent of the ticket sales, while Archie and Bill got the rest. From their share of the profits, they paid the radio station for advertising their show, plus their musicians and expenses. They went to the dates in two cars, Archie, Bill, Chet, Lowell and Mrs. Blanchard in one vehicle, the musicians in the other car.

By 1942, Archie, Bill and Chet were making personal appearances almost every night. They opened the show with a few songs together, then Archie and Bill would go backstage to dress as Grandpappy and Hot Shot Elmer, while Chet played solos and sang. The road shows took them all over Eastern Tennessee, Western Kentucky and into North Carolina.

Archie and Bill liked the Colonel's Cafe in Middlesboro, Kentucky, mainly for the slot machines. They lost so much money; however, that each time they played, they made a pact with each other never to play again. That pact fell apart each time they stopped there.

Bill Carlisle always called Chet Atkins "Smaggie." That was started by Archie, on stage at the *Merry-Go-Round*. Archie asked Chet, "What was the name of that song you played?," and Chet answered, *"S Maggie,"* meaning

"It's Maggie." Archie asked "S'maggie?" The audience laughed loudly. Chet was always "Smaggie" after that to Archie and Bill.

Campbell kept the props he used for his comedy act in a large suitcase. He felt his act was the whole show. It smelled of the spirit gum he used to glue on his whiskers for his Grandpappy act. Archie was a man of many talents. He was able to get all the guys on the *Merry-Go-Round* free passes to the Roxy Theater, where the girlie shows were held. One night, at a show in Cherokee, North Carolina, Archie nearly caused a riot. He bragged he was a ladies' man. He asked the women in the audience to raise their hands if he had not kissed them. All hands went up. Campbell then ran through the audience kissing all the women. That angered the men. A fight broke out and there was a free-for-all for about three minutes.

Archie suddenly found out his fiddle player didn't show up right before show time. Always resourceful, Archie knew that a fiddle player, Smokey White, was frying hamburgers across the street from WNOX. Archie ran across the street and hired White just in time for the show.

In 1941, Archie joined the Navy. WNOX gave a big going away party for Archie at the Regis Cafe. Songwriter Arthur Q. Smith was there "holding forth" to a large group of people. Archie walked up and immediately said, "You're crazy for selling your songs for fifty dollars." Everybody laughed, but Arthur Q., who quickly replied, "Wait a minute, you don't know how many songs I've sold for fifty dollars." Everybody was still laughing, when someone goosed Arthur Q. from behind. Chet was standing right behind him, and as Arthur Q. jumped back, he fell on Chet. Chet fell flat on his face. Archie and the crowd really laughed then.

At the end of the war, Archie returned to WNOX. In 1952, however, he left for WNOX's rival, WROL. Television had also arrived and Archie started Knoxville's first country music TV show on WROL-TV, *Country Playhouse*. That show premiered in 1952 and ended in 1958.

At that point, Archie Campbell felt he was ready for the big time. In 1958, he moved to Nashville to replace rube comic Rod Brasfield on *The Prince Albert* segment of the Opry. He also signed with RCA Records, and his recordings "Trouble In the Amen Corner" and "The Men In My Little Girl's Life" reached near *Billboard's* Top Twenty country chart. Always humorous, he loved Spoonerisms (unintentional interchanges of sounds) and in his case, Cinderella became "Rindercella," and he changed "dropped her slipper" into "Slopped her dripper." Audiences loved it. The CMA named him Comic of the Year in 1969.

Former Crazy Tennessean Roy Acuff always said that Archie would become a big star one day because of his comedy, not because of his singing. Nonetheless, he did chart some serious duets with Lorene Mann in the late 1960s, notably "Dark End Of the Street" and "My Special Prayer."

Archie became best known for TV's *Hee Haw* variety series, where he was chief writer and star comic in specialty skits, such as the cigar-chomping barber who dished up the dirt. His interchanges with fellow humorist Gordie Tapp were memorable, notably those that ended with *"Pftt, she was gone!"* He also hosted TNN's 1984 interview program *Yesteryear.*

Archie Campbell excelled in both music and comedy and was also a songwriter and a painter of note. He painted everything from landscapes to caricatures. He possessed an earthy humor. He was once known as "The Mayor Of Bulls Gap," and enjoyed golf, and was an accomplished amateur golfer.

People have a lot of good memories about Archie. DJ James Perry remembers when they used to stretch a sheet on the courthouse in Maynardville to show movies. Archie and a band would go there and perform in-between shows. The charge was twenty-five cents per person, when they could afford it.

Campbell suffered a fatal heart attack on August 29, 1987 at age seventy-two. Survivors include his wife Mary and sons Steven and Phillip. He is buried at Glenwood Cemetery near Powell, in Knox County, Tennessee. Following his death, U.S. Highway 11-E, running through Bulls Gap, was renamed Archie Campbell Highway, in his memory.

"I searched the world over
And thought I found true love,
She met another and
P-f-t-t she was gone."
Archie Campbell, Hee Haw TV

Archie Campbell

11 CLIFF CARLISLE ...

"After the war was over
I was comin' home to you
I saw a rainbow at midnight
Out on the ocean blue . . ."

Lost John Miller (Arthur Q. Smith)

Cliff Carlisle became a well known country star in the 1920s. He was born in a log cabin atop Mount Eden, near Taylorsville, Kentucky on May 6, 1903. He remembered many cold winters when the snow came through the cracks in the logs. He was born on a sharecropper's farm; half the tobacco crop went to the owner. He walked about three miles to school. In doing so, he had to cross a river and if the river rose, he had to stay with a neighbor until the waters receded. It was ten miles to the nearest grocery and when they had to go there, they rode in a buggy.

As a teenager, Cliff fused gospel, blues, Hawaiian and mountain music into a highly individual sound. Initially enamored of early Hawaiian guitar recordings, Cliff bought every record featuring the steel guitar that he could find. He also listened to black guitarists around the Spencer County Courthouse in Taylorsville. Early on, Cliff inserted a "steel nut" under the strings of his four dollar and ninety-five cents Sears guitar which gave him a Dobro sound. Cliff said, "My music is a cross between hillbilly and blues."

Cliff's performing career began at age sixteen when he teamed up with a cousin, Lillian Truax, playing socials and local talent contests. They broke up the act when Lillian married. Cliff then teamed up with a Louisville construction worker, Wilbur Ball, and the Carlisle-Ball duo began touring with vaudeville troupes and in tent shows. Cliff and Wilbur were probably the first "blue yodeling" duo.

Carlisle learned to yodel from studying Jimmie Rodgers. Cliff and Wilbur had a Hawaiian act in Louisville, and even played in vaudeville on the B. F. Keith Circuit. As Cliff recalled, "We drifted with the trend of the times." Early in 1924, Cliff recorded for Gennett Records in Richmond, Indiana. After a number of recordings, Cliff described their recording process: "There were no microphones. You sang into a big horn, shaped like a funnel, with a needle on the end for recording."

Following music trends, he changed from Hawaiian to yodeling to hobo tunes. He also worked in a string band with J. E. and Wade Mainer; then played bluegrass, before it was even labeled as such. His story cuts across almost all lines of musical entertainment in the 1920s and '30s. After that, he went strictly into hillbilly or country music.

In 1931, Carlisle recorded for the American Record Company (ARC). W. R. Calloway, from American, got Cliff a spot at WBT-Charlotte, North Carolina. During the 1930s, Cliff recorded for Decca with his band, The Buckle Busters, also adding younger brother Bill. By the late 1930s, the brothers were at WSOC-Charlotte, and having a rough time of it: "We didn't make no fortune."

50

Then Cliff and Bill moved to Charleston, West Virginia, appearing on WCHS-Charleston's show, *The Old Farm Hour*. At the time, it was so bad they called it the "Hillbilly Graveyard." This was their low point and both agreed that was not where they wanted to be. In 1940, they landed a permanent slot on *The Mid-Day Merry-Go-Round*. Cliff made the deal, one of the best the brothers ever made, staying at WNOX for thirteen years.

In 1946, The Carlisles recorded "Rainbow At Midnight," on King Records, and it scored Top Five nationally. It became a Top 10 record. King called them The Carlisle Brothers. The following month, Ernest Tubb covered their record and took his version to number one for Decca. That song was the creation of Arthur Q. Smith, who sold his rights to a Knoxville radio personality, Lost John Miller.

Cliff & Bill Carlisle

When the Carlisle Brothers joined *The Merry-Go-Round*, their original group included Claude Boone, Sonny Boy Tommy (Cliff's son), Joe Cook and Leon Scott. Boone left to join Carl Story and His Rambling Mountaineers. While on the road, Cliff and Bill both did comedy routines. Once Cliff got to cutting up in a really big way on stage, and their dressing room at this venue was only make-shift, a couple blankets hanging over a wire strung across the back of the stage. Cliff accidentally kicked the blankets down and there stood Leon Scott naked as a jaybird . . . a real showstopper!

Along about 1950, an unfortunate incident occurred at a Carlisle Brothers' concert. While doing their routine, an audience member began heckling Cliff, who stopped the show and said, "Sir, don't do that! The people who paid to get in here want to see the show. If you keep that up, we'll have to put you out." Cliff then continued the act, saying, "Now Hot Shot,

51

what're you doing' back there?" This time the heckler yelled, "None of your business!" At that point, Cliff laid down his guitar and started after the man, and Bill followed. Cliff got the guy in a hammerlock, as Bill yelled, "Cliff, don't kill him!" The man had a knife. But Bill held Cliff until the law came and took the man away and he dropped the knife.

That experience left Cliff shaken and on the way home, he told his brother, "I'm gonna have to hang it up, it's getting next to me." Indeed, Cliff never did play the road again, though he still did some recording. In 1951, he retired from WNOX. Bill stayed on, working with acts like Martha Carson, Eddie Hill and Archie Campbell.

In his retirement, Cliff used his talent as an artist. He did oil paintings, mostly scenic works of historical places and things. Cliff was among the first country pickers to use the resonator guitar, originally made by the Dopyera brothers in Los Angeles. This is the guitar that became known as the Dobro. Cliff cut over three hundred sides in the 1930s and '40s, and claimed to have written some five hundred songs. He was one of the most historically significant performers, a pioneer in the use of the steel guitar and the Dobro. (Cliff Carlisle died April 5, 1983, of a heart attack in Lexington, Kentucky, at age seventy-nine).

12 BILL CARLISLE ...
Hot Shot Elmer

William Toliver Carlisle was born December 19, 1908, in a little old farmhouse in Briar Ridge, Kentucky. When he was ten, the Carlisles moved to Louisville. Bill had four brothers, Lewis, Milton, Marion, Cliff, and two sisters, Henrietta and Regina. They all loved to sing, in church or anywhere. Bill purchased his first guitar in 1923, a Silvertone brand, from Sears & Roebuck. A kindly friend next door taught him a few chords.

The first song Bill ever wrote was "Rattlesnake Daddy," a yodel tune, while at WLAP-Lexington, Kentucky, where he appeared on *The Carlisle Family Jamboree*. Recorded in 1933 on Vocalion Records, "Rattlesnake Daddy" boasted a Jimmie Rodgers feel to it, as Rodgers was Bill's idol at that time. When Bill began working with brother Cliff, they moved from station to station and were a featured act on WSB-Atlanta's *Barn Dance*.

Then in 1940, Lowell Blanchard offered them a spot on the WNOX *Mid-Day Merry Go-Round,* which lasted a baker's dozen years. Their segment was sponsored by Scalf's Indian River Tonic. It was there Bill developed his comedy character "Hot Shot Elmer." He would appear on stage first as Bill Carlisle and then go back stage and dress as Hot Shot Elmer. Bill did this for about two years before audiences realized he was not two people. Hot Shot Elmer was a barefoot rube comic, who seemed to be constantly changing from flashy western costumes to a country rube garb. The mail poured in by the bushel for pictures of Hot Shot Elmer, so Bill had pictures made in his Hot Shot Elmer costumes. He studied and practiced a wide variety of mannerisms and character traits for the act.

Their sponsor changed from Scalf to the American Brick Siding Company. One memorable night, Hot Shot ate a whole onion, pretending it was an apple; however, tears streamed down his face as he told a sad story. The sadder the story got, the more Elmer cried and the more the crowd laughed.

Lowell Blanchard wrote a lot of jokes in the scripts. One had Hot Shot Elmer sitting on duck eggs. Well, it takes twenty-one days to hatch a duck egg. As Hot Shot Elmer sat there on the nest, barefoot, Blanchard would ask, "How's the ducks comin' on?" Imitating an irritable duck sitting on a nest, Elmer said, "Don't mess with me, 'cause I'm mean when I'm settin'!" Then he would say, "I hear 'em peckin'! Won't be long now."

They carried this on for twenty-one days. The day they were supposed to hatch, Bill brought in baby ducks to the studio and put them in the nest. Blanchard was at the mic and Bill went up to him and said, "I do believe we've got some ducks today." Blanchard looked and said, "Yeah! Footfire! They're out of their shells." Then he picked up a duck next to the mic, and the duck obligingly "Quack! Quacked!" The baby ducks, thinking Bill was their mother, started following him all over the stage, leaving a hazardous mess. When Lowell complained, Bill pinned tiny diapers on their bottoms. The ducks were such a hit that Blanchard, Bill and Archie

Campbell even took the ducks with them on personal appearances. Bill acknowledged, "That gimmick really drew a crowd."

When Bill and Cliff recorded "Rainbow At Midnight" on King Records, it became the biggest hit the brothers had together. In the early 1950s when Cliff quit the act, Bill continued at *The Merry-Go-Round* with his own group, under the name The Carlisles. After Cliff left, Bill toured with such talents as Martha Carson and Archie Campbell. He and Archie even did some comedy wrestling matches on stage, and gave unknown musician Chet Atkins his first job at WNOX, playing fiddle.

Bill toured with sisters Minnie (Woodruff) and Martha Carson.

Bill was still with WNOX when he cut "Too Old To Cut the Mustard" in July 1951 for Mercury Records. As "Too Old . . ." producer D. Kilpatrick and publisher Fred Rose encouraged WSM to invite Bill and his frequent touring partner Martha Carson, who has just scored with her gospel composition "Satisfied," to audition. They both guested on the Prince Albert segment, and the Opry's Jim Denny, then director of WSM's Artists Service Bureau, asked Bill to stay over; however, Carlisle went back to Knoxville, giving notice to Blanchard at WNOX. When three weeks passed and no word from Denny, he called Jim to determine when he was to report to the *Opry*? Instead, Denny told him they weren't going to put him on right then.

A proud man, Bill wouldn't tell Lowell he had been turned down by the Opry, so he started writing letters to other shows, but all replied they weren't hiring just then. That inspired Bill to write a novelty number "No Help Wanted," which became a smash. When "No Help Wanted" skyrocketed into number one on the chart, KWKH-Shreveport called, wanting The Carlisles for their *Louisiana Hayride*. So Bill went to KWKH. Later, when the *Opry* called wanting him, Bill, knowing they had taken Martha instead of him, refused their offer. He stayed at the *Hayride* nearly two years. After WSM called twice more, he finally accepted their offer, joining the *Grand Ole Opry* on November 14, 1953.

But Bill retired Hot Shot Elmer when he went to the Opry. He didn't have a straight man and besides, the show's tight schedule and brief time allotted artists, didn't allow time necessary to do the comedy build-up needed. Yet, Bill's Opry membership lasted forty-nine years, making his last appearance on the show two weeks prior to his death on March 17, 2003 (at age ninety-four). Incidentally, for the record, that final night he sang "Jack Of All Trades" and "Worried Man Blues."

In September 2002, rather belatedly, singer-songwriter-guitarist-co-median Bill Carlisle was elected into the Country Music Hall of Fame, along with another Opry great, Porter Wagoner. Bill was often quoted saying, "Things change, but I just keep shuckin' the same old corn." Of his Knoxville days, he said, "Those of us who were fortunate enough to land a spot on *The Mid-Day Merry-Go-Round* or *The Tennessee Barn Dance*, only thought of it as an opportunity to earn a living, doing what we loved best. If we moved on to other venues, it was for more money or just because it sounded like fun. We lived and we worked. That's what ordinary people do. Every person on earth contributes something that will become history."

13 MARTHA CARSON...

Martha Carson was born Irene Ethel Amburgey, on May 19, 1921, near Neon, Kentucky. She grew up in a musical clan in the Great Smoky Mountains, dancing to the tunes of her forefathers. She became steeped in the traditional music she heard at home. From those beginnings, music became a vital part of Martha's life. She learned to play an old fashioned two pedal organ when she was ten years old. By the time she was fourteen, she got her first guitar, by trading her pet calf for that instrument. Music and entertaining just came naturally to Martha and her sisters Bertha Mae and Opal Jean.

Martha was truly a coal-miner's daughter. Her father was a "brattice man" for the Elkhorn Coal Company. That meant he designed and constructed wooden support framework inside the mines. With his wife Gertrude and other family members, they performed throughout the area in a gospel group.

The sisters began their singing career as The Sunshine Sisters on local radio, then John Lair engaged them to substitute singers in his Coon Creek Girls (with Lily May Ledford), before launching The Hoot Owl Holler Girls, with the sisters portraying Minnie, Marthie and Mattie at WSB-Atlanta.

It was in 1939, Martha met James (Roberts) Carson in Lexington, Kentucky. He was good looking and just out of the Navy. James literally swept her off her feet. He, too, was musically inclined (as his father was known throughout the area as Fiddlin' Doc Roberts), and their shared love of music brought them close. By 1940, they were married. James wanted to sing duets with Martha; he sang the lead and she sang tenor. James also played mandolin, and Martha accompanied on guitar.

After "paying their dues" at WHIS-Bluefield, West Virginia, *The Renfro Valley Barn Dance* and other radio stations, Martha and James became part of WSB-Atlanta's *Barn Dance*, which had debuted on November 16, 1940. James and Martha were staff members there for nine years, and their popularity as a duo earned them the title, *Barn Dance Sweethearts*. Atlanta, at that time was a great country music area and became a prime distribution center for major record labels like RCA Victor.

The *Barn Dance Sweethearts* also recorded as James & Martha Carson for Capitol Records, but soon the *Sweethearts* name came to be a joke. James started hanging out at bars and before long his other-women affairs began to be known among their fellow artists.

James began saying hateful things to Martha, which hurt her deeply. They stayed together because of her faith and their duet status on the *Barn Dance,* even when James became so verbally and at times even physically abusive. Martha suggested divorce, but James said, "I don't want no damned divorce." Their marriage was stormy, and in its February 18, 1950 edition, the trade journal *Billboard* announced: "James and Martha Carson recently moved from WSB-Atlanta to WNOX-Knoxville."

56

James and Martha moved to Knoxville to perform on *The Mid-Day Merry-Go-Round* and Saturday night's *Tennessee Barn Dance*. On the *Barn Dance,* WNOX continued to call them "Barn Dance Sweethearts." Martha hoped the change of venue would help their marriage. Instead, things went from bad to worse, until one day, Martha could stand no more. She told Lowell Blanchard and friend and fellow entertainer Bill Carlisle, she was leaving the show, and was off the show for about three months.

Then one day, Blanchard summoned Martha to come back. In 1950, Martha got a divorce, and Blanchard gave James his "walking papers." *Billboard* announced in its April 28, 1951 issue: "James and Martha Carson have split. She is working with Bill Carlisle at WNOX-Knoxville." Martha had never really sung by herself before. She sang harmony with her sisters in a trio, or duets with James. In fact, she was frightened of singing solo, but Blanchard encouraged her, "Martha, you've got more talent than you realize. Stay on and give yourself a chance." Of course, she did.

During 1951, Martha began traveling with Bill Carlisle, her sister (Jean) Mattie O'Neil & Salty Holmes, plus fiddler Sandy Sandusky, in between their shows at WNOX. Martha recalled that Bill Carlisle was the funniest man she had ever met: "Bill would go into a restaurant and empty the toothpick holder, putting the toothpicks in his pocket. When I asked him why he did that, he would say, 'My daddy runs a lumber company and I'm trying to run the price up.'" Martha added that he was a miracle man, who could write comedy songs like "Too Old To Cut The Mustard," then write a heartfelt song like "Gone Home" (which Bill's good friend Grandpa Jones later cut).

This period, after divorcing James and being so afraid of singing alone, was a sad time for Martha. At this low ebb in her life, while riding out on the road, sitting in the back seat of Carlisle's car, she wrote her biggest hit. She said God spoke to her, saying, "I'm satisfied, and you're satisfied," then frantically looked around for something to write on and found a dirty blank check on the car's floor. Wiping it off as best she could, Martha wrote down the lyrics to "Satisfied," as she was inspired to do: *"Satisfied, satisfied / No troubles can ever get me down / For when my eyes are closed in death / With my Jesus, I'll be at rest / Then you'll know, I'm satisfied . . ."*

Capitol A&R chief Ken Nelson recorded Martha singing "Satisfied" at Castle Studios in Nashville, November 5, 1951. Jean, her husband Salty Holmes and Bill Carlisle provided the harmony. Despite her wariness, it only took three takes to record her hit record. Musicians Chet Atkins played lead guitar; Ernie Newton was on bass; Harold Bradley, rhythm guitar; and Marvin Hughes played piano, all helped produce this classic gospel recording. Released December 10, 1951, "Satisfied" became a Gold Record for Capitol, and a much in-demand request on radio.

The record was so hot that WSM's Jack Stapp, program director, asked Martha to guest on *The Grand Ole Opry*. Martha, of course, was still on WNOX, but audiences loved her upbeat, lively vocals, which led to an invitation to join the Opry on April 12, 1952.

When Martha went back to Knoxville to say good-bye, she dreaded telling Blanchard and all her friends in the cast, but was pleased that they all sincerely wished her well. Martha always said she felt blessed to have been a part of the 1950s' *Mid-Day Merry-Go-Round* and to have been able to work with producer Lowell Blanchard. On April 15, 1952, *Billboard* confirmed the news officially: "Martha Carson has joined *The Grand Ole Opry*."

In 1953, Martha married promoter, Xavier (X) Cosse. He promoted her toward a more pop-oriented market, and urged her change from Capitol to RCA. The couple moved to New York for a while, even departing the *Opry*, while appearing on national TV shows and playing the supper club circuit.

Martha Carson had proved a great asset to *The Merry-Go-Round*, as a vocal stylist and an inspired songwriter. As *Tonight Show* host Steve Allen once proclaimed, "Martha Carson is not just a singer, she's an explosion!" Chet Atkins added, "She's the best entertainer I've ever seen," citing a tremendous amount of energy.

Fiery-haired Martha died at age eighty-three on December 16, 2004. Peter Cooper, then staff writer for *The Tennessean* daily newspaper in Nashville, called her the "Rockin' Queen of Happy Spirituals."

Martha recording with Buddy Harman and Harold Bradley.

14 THE CARTERS...

"Will the Circle Be Unbroken..."

The Original Carter Family (A.P. Carter, his wife Sara, and Sara's cousin, Maybelle), were from Poor Valley in the southwest corner of Virginia, bordering on Tennessee. In July 1927, they auditioned for RCA's Ralph Peer in Bristol, Tennessee, for a historic field recording session. From that point on, the trio recorded on a fairly regular basis until 1941. Songs like "Keep On the Sunny Side" and "The Wildwood Flower" became Carter standards. A.P. rarely sang and didn't play an instrument. When the spirit moved him, he'd join in with what he called "bassin' in." Maybelle usually sang harmony to Sara's lead vocals, and played guitar with what was called the "Carter lick." She also played autoharp and banjo.

Maybelle Addington was born May 10, 1909 in Nickelsville, Virginia. She married Ezra (Eck) Carter on March 13, 1926, when she was sixteen years old. Eck was A.P.'s brother. Maybelle and Eck had three daughters, Helen Myrl, Valerie June, and Ina Anita. When the original Carter Family split up, Maybelle's daughters joined her to form a new group and sound: Mother Maybelle & The Carter Sisters.

"Pop" Carter (Eck) was probably the first to recognize how far Maybelle's talent could take them. He grew more excited about her career than her, especially after seeing Carter Family records being sold in towns up and down the railroad line on which he worked as a railway mail clerk. Besides he always seemed to be looking for a way out of Poor Valley, Virginia, which he felt was well named.

Maybelle, with her three girls, Helen, June and Anita, tried settling down, but after six months. Pop Carter said, "Go out and find a place to sing. I can't stand to see your long face anymore. If the money is good, take it. The mountains will always be here." So the three teen-age girls became full time musicians, though Helen was the most capable musician, Anita the finest singer, and June the best showman.

With Helen on accordion, June on autoharp and Anita on bass, Mother Maybelle hit the airwaves out of WRVA-Richmond, Virginia in 1943. The transition from old-timey Carter Family trio to the new sound of an all-female band was gradual. Maybelle introduced her daughters to show business during a radio stint in Charlotte, North Carolina. By this time, the Carter name had national renown. Between singing the old Carter Family songs, they sang pop tunes. They did vaudeville-style skits and sold pictures for twenty-five cents apiece. By 1946, they became a big draw on Richmond's *Old Dominion Barn Dance*.

Then, in 1948, The Carter Sisters and Mother Maybelle, as they were billed, went over to Knoxville to work *The Mid-Day Merry-Go-Round.* and *The Tennessee Barn Dance*. They proved an instant success, as crowds flocked into the auditorium to see them. The lines were so long at the Saturday night

Barn Dance that you had to plan to come early to get in. Pop soon had them booked all over, and then asked Chet Atkins to join them. As Chet noted, "We traveled further in a new Frazier auto than I'd ever been before." They played the Saturday night *Barn Dance*, then headed for a Sunday show at some far-flung spot like in Roanoke or a park in Pennsylvania. Pop liked to drive at a hundred miles an hour, but Maybelle would caution him, "Now Daddy, don't drive so fast. We want to get there." After the show, they would drive back to play *The Merry-Go-Round* at noon on Monday.

When they got a call from KWTO's *Ozark Jubilee*, they wired they would accept the offer. There were all kinds of towns to work in the Midwest, including Tulsa, Little Rock, St. Louis and Kansas City. The Carter Sisters, Mother Maybelle and Chet Atkins all joined the *Jubilee* in Springfield, late in 1949, staying there about a year, until they were invited to join the Opry cast a year later.

When the Carters moved to Nashville, they all boarded at Mom Upchurch's Boarding House, at 620 Boscobel Street. Don Davis, steel player with Pee Wee King, talked all his fellow borders at Mom's into doubling up to make room for them. (Don, who later married and divorced Anita, and again married and divorced Anita, slept on a couch in the living room.) Chet, with his wife and daughter, toughed it out in a non-air-conditioned apartment, also in East Nashville. The Carters were the only females to ever board at Mom's.

In 1955, the Carters joined a package tour starring Hank Snow, The Louvin Brothers and an also added attraction, young Elvis Presley. Howard White, playing steel with Snow, said, "I will always remember how Presley's gyrating had the girls squealing, all new to country artists." It was reported that Anita Carter loved Presley's act and he also got a crush on her.

Mother Maybelle (from left), Helen, Howard White, Anita and June Carter backstage at WNOX, 1951.

Everywhere they went, the Carters were well received. They had tremendous drawing power as the Original Carter Family was still remembered fondly. Even with all this popularity, the Carter sisters began to lose interest. The girls each got married and each pursued other interests. Mother Maybelle was unhappy about the act falling apart, but years later, they reunited when June married Johnny Cash. So once more the Carter Sisters and Mother Maybelle sang together, touring frequently with Cash. From 1968 onward, they were regular performers on Cash's weekly network variety show, which ran to 1971. (By then Johnny and June were Mr. and Mrs.)

In 1970, Maybelle was inducted into the Country Music Hall Of Fame, as part of The Original Carter Family. Mother Maybelle died October 23, 1978. Her death was the subject of Johnny's song, "Tears In The Holston River." Helen died June 2, 1998 and Anita's death followed on July 29, 1999. June died May 15, 2003. Pop and Maybelle Carter, and their daughters, are buried in Hendersonville Memory Gardens at Hendersonville, Tennessee. The circle is again unbroken.

15 COWBOY COPAS . . .
A Waltz King

His parents named him Lloyd Estel Copas. Fans knew him as "The Oklahoma Cowboy" or "Cowboy" Copas. His wife Lucille called him "Cope." WSM announcer Ott Devine called him "The Best-Dressed Dressed Man From the West." It could be said the "Waltz King" title fit him best. He was the second artist to cut "Tennessee Waltz," co-writer Pee Wee King being the first.

The story that Copas publicized to all the world was that he was born in Muskogee, Oklahoma. Most of his public believed him, but the folks in Adams County, Ohio, near Blue Creek, knew better. Lloyd Copas was born on July 15, 1913 at the Cameron Place in Cameron Hollow near Blue Creek, Ohio.

As an entertainer, Copas felt that if he was going to be a cowboy he needed the Oklahoma background to enhance his career. He told his family, "I'd rather be an Oklahoma cowboy than an Ohio ridge runner." Copas' family played music for local barn dances around the home area. When Copas was fourteen, he played guitar with a string band called The Hen Cacklers. When sixteen, he met up with fiddler Vernon Storer, who billed himself as "Natchee The Indian." They claimed that Copas grew up on an Oklahoma ranch, met an Indian named "Natchee" and they teamed up to perform together. Great teaming! The Cowboy and the Indian!

Before going to Knoxville Copas played at WCHS-Charleston, West Virginia and at WLW and WKRC in Cincinnati. In 1940, Copas became a member of *The Mid-Day Merry-Go-Round*. At that time, Carl Story, Carl Smith, Sunshine Slim Sweet, Molly O'Day and Elton Britt were also part of the WNOX show. Natchee was really quite good as a fiddle back-up for Copas. When asked how he was, he would always say, "Busier than a one-legged man at an ass kickin'!"

When Natchee decided to leave, Copas hired fiddler Bob Steele. Copas also had Woody Woodruff on bass and Shorty Sharp on guitar. Like others, they not only worked the *Merry-Go-Round*, but played venues in and around Knoxville. At their shows, they sold boxes of candy, weighing three-fourths of an ounce for fifty cents. Supposedly, one box would have a diamond ring in it for the lucky recipient.

Copas always liked "characters," and liked having one on his show. Little Moses, The Human Lodestone, only weighed ninety-seven pounds and was also very short. He could stand and extend both arms, and a man would reach under each arm and try to lift him. For some reason, no one could, yet somebody from the audience would always try.

When Copas came to Knoxville, he was singing "The Tragic Romance," a natural hit for *The Merry-Go-Round* crowd. Its first line proclaimed, *"Nestled in the heart of the Tennessee hills . . ."* and Knoxville was indeed nestled in the heart of the Tennessee Hills.

At the start of 1943, Cowboy Copas left WNOX, but didn't go to Nashville at that time, as so many did. Instead, he returned to WKRC-Cincinnati, and while there recorded "Filipino Baby" for Syd Nathan's King Records. It became a Top Five record in 1946. Copas also replaced Eddy Arnold in Pee Wee's Golden West Cowboys, when Eddy set out on his own. After doing a few guest spots on *The Grand Ole Opry,* Copas became a bona fide cast member in the fall of '46, when announcer Grant Turner dubbed him, "The Waltz King Of The Grand Ole Opry."

Cope was in Kansas City on March 5, 1963, with a star-studded show to benefit the widow of DJ Jack Call, who had died in a recent auto accident. Following their performance, Copas, Patsy Cline and Hawkshaw Hawkins were passengers in a small plane piloted by Copas' son-in-law Randy Hughes, flying home. Around seven p.m. that date, the plane dove into the hard, cold, winter woods in a thunderstorm near Camden, Tennessee, some eighty-five miles west of Nashville. There were no survivors. "Goodbye Kisses," a near Top Ten prophetic swan song by Copas (which he co-wrote with Lefty Frizzell) would peak in late Spring 1963.

Oddly enough, the myth of Lloyd "Cowboy" Copas' birthplace extended unto death, as his death certificate read: "Birthplace - Oklahoma." That information was given by his widow Lucille. Thus his family protected his need to be an Oklahoma Cowboy even to the end.

Cowboy Copas

16 DON GIBSON ...

"A Legend in his own time."

Donald Eugene Gibson was born April 3, 1928, in Shelby, North Carolina, to a railroad man and his wife, neither of whom had much interest in music. Don's dad died when he was two years old. While he was in second grade, he just stopped going to school and nobody cared. At fourteen, Don bought himself a cheap guitar and started hanging out with regular guitar pickers. The older guys taught him chords, licks and runs. Then at sixteen, he and Ned Costner put a band together with Jim Barber, fiddle and trumpet, Howard Sisk, rhythm guitar, Hal (Pee Wee) Peeke, electric guitar, and Milton Scarborough, accordion. Don sang and played bass. The boys called themselves Sons Of the Soil.

In 1948, they landed a slot at Shelby's radio station, WHOS. In 1949, Mercury Records was anxious to get into the hillbilly market and had just hired Murray Nash as its new country A&R chief. Nash had heard Sons Of the Soil on the radio, and he set up a session with them. On his way to Shelby, he stopped at WBT-Charlotte, North Carolina, where he picked up two songs from Claude Casey.

In the Spring of 1949, Nash recorded Casey's two songs plus two others provided by Sons Of the Soil. They recorded at WBBO-Forest City, North Carolina. Those marked Gibson's first recordings and they fizzled.

Before long, Sons Of the Soil broke up, and Don struck out on his own. He formed a new band calling

Don with Wade Ray at WNOX, 1950.

them King Cotton Kinfolks, comprising Blackie Lunsford, fiddle; Billy Kirby, bass; Summie Lee (Eagle Eye) Hendrick, steel guitar; and Seth Addis, guitar. This time, Don, wanting to record again, contacted Steve Sholes at RCA, who set up a session for October 17, 1950 at WSOC-Charlotte. Those recordings sold like Mercury's had, not at all.

Don was becoming frustrated. There was an announcer in Shelby who told Don about WNOX- Knoxville's shows *The Mid-Day Merry-Go-Round* and *The Tennessee Barn Dance*. He told Don, "There is a community of songwriters there, and if you could get on WNOX, it would be the best place to go." Don went to WNOX on a Saturday night in 1950 to audition, taking his band with him. Lowell Blanchard hired him at thirty dollars a week.

Blanchard introduced his new star, saying, "Here's the young man with the fine voice and fantastic phrasing. He adds the modern touch to our music here." Don went over well on radio, but his smooth style didn't go over as well at live venues. He found himself at a time in country music when there was a shift between the old venue of schoolhouses and small town auditoriums, to night clubs and dance halls. RCA recorded him again in 1951, but those recordings did not do well and his contract was not renewed.

Gibson was still on the *Merry-Go-Round* with a new band; Howard White, steel guitar, Marion Sumner, fiddle, Luke Brandon, guitar, and Billy Kirby, bass. They recorded a demo session at WBIR, which Don sent to a promoter in Nashville, Troy Martin. Troy set up a session at Castle Studios in the Tulane Hotel, Nashville, July 7, 1952 for Don and his band. They recorded four songs: "No Shoulder To Cry On," "We're Stepping Out Tonight," "Sample Kisses" and "Let Me Stay In Your Arms." Troy added to the band Nashville session players Grady Martin, guitar and Marvin Hughes, piano.

Don Law, A&R at Columbia, signed Gibson to a contract on July 26, 1952, for a two per-cent royalty rate. Columbia released two singles, but neither hit. By 1955, Don was becoming more and more frustrated. He had been married to a real sweet gal, Beth. Then he left her for a girl he met at the Blue Circle hamburger joint, and that marriage didn't work too well.

To further complicate life, that summer WNOX moved from its long time Gay Street site to new digs at Willow Springs. The new location had a big empty basement, and as Don said, "It had interesting acoustics." A year prior, Don had written a song, "I'm Glad I Got To See You Once Again," which Hank Snow recorded and when released in 1955, became a Top Ten single. Don figured if he had written one hit, maybe he could write another. One day after a show, he was sitting in that oddly acoustic basement and started humming a melody. Then he came up with the lyrics, and before he knew it, he had created that hit he wanted so badly, "Sweet Dreams."

Gibson began singing at Esslinger's, a club on the Alcoa Highway, just across from the old airport. He started singing "Sweet Dreams" there. One night while in the Knoxville area, Nashville publisher Wesley Rose dropped by for a beer, heard Don and his "Sweet Dreams." Well, the rest is musical history. Wesley discovered Don just like dad Fred Rose discovered Hank Williams. Acuff-Rose contracted for "Sweet Dreams" and soon wrangled Gibson a recording deal at MGM, former home to Hank Williams.

Don cut his first sides for MGM, September 12, 1955, and though it charted Top Ten on August 11, 1956, the single dropped off *Billboard* after a week. Don mused that they had insisted he sing like Hank Williams, not his style at all. But the good news for Gibson was that Faron Young covered his disc on Capitol, made it a near number one chart song, and it remained on *Billboard's* country chart thirty-three weeks, earning Don and Acuff-Rose a nice chunk of change, and established Gibson as a writer to respect.

So Don decided to leave WNOX, moving to WWVA's *Wheeling Jamboree* in West Virginia, but when that didn't pan out, returned to Knoxville, now broke and living at the Shilom Trailer Park off Clinton Highway, situated back in the woods.

Fortunately for Don, Chet Atkins was engaged by RCA-Nashville in 1951. Chet hadn't forgotten Gibson's formidable talents and as the new head of RCA's country division in '57, invited Don back to Nashville to record. Thanks to Chet's initiative, Don became a hot new singer, as well as a critically-acclaimed songwriter, as they produced a series of hits, five in a row in 1958, all penned by Gibson: "Oh Lonesome Me," "I Can't Stop Loving You," "Blue Blue Day," "Give Myself a Party" and "Look Who's Blue." Both "Oh Lonesome Me" and "Blue Blue Day" reached number one and the others Top Ten or better. That was a stunning introduction to the world for this relative newcomer.

In 1958, Don was asked to become a member of the prestigious *Grand Ole Opry*, and so he moved to Nashville and literally became like the song he wrote "(A) Legend In My Time" (which went number one for Ronnie Milsap in 1975).

Being by nature, a shy man, the business of being a star got to Don. Sometime in 1960, he began having problems with drinking and narcotics, and let his career slide. It seemed he simply didn't care anymore, and was fired by the Opry in 1963, after showing up two hours late to emcee the network *Prince Albert Show*.

A new wife in 1967, Bobbi Patterson, saved him and his career. Don himself credited her with adding stability to his life, and help him overcome his problems. Old friend Wesley Rose came back into the picture, as well, and in 1970, Rose began producing Gibson on his Hickory Records label.

Guest artist (possibly) Mattie O'Neil performs as Gibson's band waits their turn (from left) Don seated, Howard White standing and Blackie Lunsford, at the Mid-Day Merry-Go-Round in 1951.

In 1971, Don took the Eddy Raven composition "Country Green" into the Top Five, and the following year hit number one again with Gary Paxton's "Woman (Sensuous Woman)," and a series of duets with pop-country artist Sue Thompson. His good luck charms Eddy Raven supplied another hit with "Touch The Morning" in 1973, and Gary Paxton's "One Day At A Time" became another Top Ten in 1974.

In 1975, Don was asked to rejoin the Opry, and Rose continued to record him on Hickory until 1984. Don even did one last session with Chet Atkins at RCA, and the final mix took place on July 12, 1986. Don, a top singer-songwriter-musician once said, "I consider myself a songwriter who sings, rather than a singer who writes songs."

Nonetheless, Don dropped out of show business after 1986, surrendering to the shadows of shyness he had fought all his life. He and Bobbi kept to themselves, and Don began suffering a decline in health. In 2001, Gibson was inducted into the Country Music Hall of Fame.

Some say he was depressed, and brooded about a career hurt by his addictions. On September 17, 2003, Don died at age seventy-five. He was buried in the family plot in Shelby, North Carolina. At long last, Don Gibson was at rest, a situation he seemingly sought all his life. Bobbi Gibson helps to keep her husband's memory alive in a museum, situated in an old theater in Shelby, his old hometown.

17 HOMER & JETHRO...
Henry Haynes and Kenneth Burns

Lowell Blanchard once kicked Henry D. Haynes and Kenneth C. Burns out of an amateur show in Knoxville, saying, "You kids ain't amateurs." After disqualifying them, he gave them jobs at WNOX.

Actually, Burns began playing professionally at age twelve with his close boyhood friend, Haynes. They formed a band they called The String Dusters, but when Blanchard forgot their name on a 1936 *Mid-Day Merry-Go-Round* show, he called them "Homer & Jethro." The name stuck. By then the boys were developing a duo style of mixing madcap humor and skillful playing, with Homer on rhythm guitar and Jethro playing mandolin.

World War II had interrupted their teaming for a time, as they served their country, Homer assigned to the Pacific and Jethro as an infantry soldier in Europe. They reunited to work on WLW-Cincinnati, and signed with King Records as staff musicians. They next developed a gimmick of parodying hit songs. Among titles they fractured were "Five Minutes More" and "Over The Rainbow."

By 1948, they were working back at WNOX and proved very popular. That's when Chet Atkins - Jethro's brother-in-law as they married twin sisters Lois and Leona Johnson - took Lowell Blanchard's suggestion to team up with them. So Chet and Leona moved to Knoxville, and lived next door

Homer & Jethro in the 1965 movie 'Second Fiddle To A Steel Guitar.'

to Lois and Jethro. The team-mates conceived an act calling it "Chet Atkins and The Colorado Mountain Boys, Featuring Homer & Jethro." In addition, they'd added Jethro's brother Aytchie on bass.

It was a good show, with Homer & Jethro playing duets and a lot of light jazzy stuff, before going into their comedy routine; however, people there didn't seem excited about their show. They tried everything, even slapstick, to put the show across, but nothing seemed to work. In those days, movie theaters featured live shows between screenings. When they played those theaters, Homer would sit in the audience during the movie and pull out a cap pistol, and jump up to help the good guys when they were cornered. The audience thought that was funny and it did help get the audience in a better frame of mind for when they did their act.

In actuality, their music was probably a little too slick for the East Tennessee audiences, mainly used to bluegrass and hoedowns. Chet became depressed, and Jethro said, "When we started playing, they didn't accept us as being funny. And we were trying to be." Radio and public appearances were fun to Homer and Jethro. Soon people began going backstage to tell them how much they liked their act. One night in Kentucky, after the curtain closed, the audience just sat there thinking there was more. Cliff Carlisle was on the show, and he finally stuck his head out through the curtains and yelled, "That's all, folks! Sure enough!"

With experience, Homer & Jethro knew exactly what the other one was going to do and the act moved smoothly. It had to, because on radio back then, they had no "canned" laughter. If a joke fell on its face, there was nothing but dead air.

When Homer & Jethro were on the WLS-Chicago *National Barn Dance*, they always did the last show. When WLS went off the air for the night, the audience erupted because they knew that Homer & Jethro were going to give them the real swinging stuff that they couldn't do on the air.

They also worked the *Grand Ole Opry* with Red Foley's *Prince Albert Show*. Nothing was going well one night and Red got nervous and started shaking so badly that he couldn't read a script he was holding. Homer just reached over and took it away from him and held it in front of Red's eyes. The audience thought it was part of the act and roared spontaneously.

In the early days, censors would cut out lines of their songs, but when they did the show live, they would sing them anyway. Early radio would try and write jokes for them. On the show, they would throw the script in the air and ad lib the rest of the show.

Once while performing on *Don McNeil's Breakfast Club* on national radio from Chicago, Don wanted the show rehearsed. Homer and Jethro refused. They didn't even have words written down for their songs. Don would go crazy with fear that they would forget them, and it did happen once, but Jethro said, "Hey, let's go back and do that again." The second time they got it right. Don said, "You had it planned, didn't you?" "Sure did," they lied.

Thanks to their popular song parodies, Homer and Jethro finally rose to fame. On King Records in early 1949, they charted their first Top 20 novelty number, one they co-wrote: "I Feel That Old Age Coming On." RCA then signed the duo, teaming them with Opry comic June Carter on their parody "Baby, It's Cold Outside" in the fall of '49, marking their first Top Ten record.

Homer & Jethro's biggest record occurred by fracturing the Patti Page hit "How Much Is that Doggie In the Window," retitled "How Much Is That Hound Dog In the Window," which peaked at number two in 1953, charting nine weeks. A highlight of their career was winning a 1959 Best Comedy Performance-Musical Grammy for "Battle of Kookamonga," their takedown of Jimmy Driftwood's Best Song Grammy winner "The Battle of New Orleans" (which also won for country singer Johnny Horton's performance). That particular parody made Home & Jethro headliners in Las Vegas.

Homer died of a heart attack, August 7, 1971, at age fifty-one. Briefly, Burns attempted to continue the act with a younger player, Ken Eidson, but that just didn't jell. Jethro kept on entertaining, though he concentrated more on his pickin' talent, with a modicum of humor to top it off. He also worked on various instrumental projects with Chet, and at educating others. A highly respected mandolinist, Jethro died of cancer on February 4, 1989, at age sixty-eight. Homer & Jethro were posthumously enshrined in the Country Music Hall of Fame in 2001.

18 SONNY JAMES...
The Southern Gentleman

"Young love, first love
Filled with true emotion,
Young love, our love,
We share with deep devotion."

Carole Joyner-Ric Cartey

Sonny James was born James Hugh Loden on May 1, 1928, in Hackleburg, Alabama. His father Archie Lee (Pop) Loden and mother Della (Burleson) Loden operated a three-hundred acre farm outside Hackleburg. His parents and older sister Thelma Lee, were all musicians. Pop played banjo, fiddle, guitar and mandolin, and his mother and sister played guitar. By age three, Sonny was singing and playing mandolin, his first instrument made by Pop from the bottom of a molasses bucket, by adding a neck, and tuning it like a mandolin.

At age four, little Sonny began his music career with Thelma on WMSD-Muscle Shoals, Alabama. Besides the Lodens, there was another Alabaman, Ruby Palmer, whom they took in as a little girl, and who later played in the Loden Family act. In 1933, The Loden Family began regular appearances on WMSD's Saturday slot.

Then they landed a daily spot on KLCN-Blytheville, Arkansas, where they provided morning music for early risers. After that they held down spots on several radio stations, throughout the South, including much later WSGN-Birmingham.

The Loden Family also affiliated with WNOX, appearing on both the *Mid-Day Merry-Go-Round* and *Tennessee Barn Dance* programs. Sonny said, "I don't remember auditioning for Lowell, so evidently he heard us somewhere." At the time, the WNOX roster included Cliff and Bill Carlisle, Archie Campbell, Johnnie Wright, Eddie Hill, Molly O'Day and Lynn Davis, and Sonny recalled that Lost John Miller worked there during the winter of 1945. Sonny became friends with Miller's banjoist Earl Scruggs. It was during the Lodens' stay at the station, Pop hired accordion player Buddy Bains.

In 1946, the family moved to WPTF-Raleigh, by now working under the billing Sonny Loden & His Southerners, and that's where Sonny struck up a friendship with Chet Atkins, then appearing with Johnnie Wright's band. Sonny said in retrospect, their stays in Knoxville and Raleigh were artistically fulfilling.

It was in 1949 that Eddie Hill, who had also been in Raleigh with Wright, encouraged Sonny to join him and the Louvin Brothers (Ira and Charlie) at WMPS-Memphis. A bass player at WMPS, John Gallaher, who had also been on the *Merry-Go-Round*, was so smitten with Sonny's sister Thelma that he grew weak in the knees whenever he saw her. Steel player

Don Davis laughed so hard, and he told Sonny about it. Sonny smiled, "That's nothing new. Every guy that comes along falls in love with her."

Following high school graduation, and with the Korean War flaring up, Sonny found himself serving fifteen months in the military, including duty in Korea. Later, Sonny played guitar on station WHBQ-Memphis, sometimes singing. In 1951, Sonny moved to Nashville. There Atkins was helpful in him signing with Ken Nelson for Capitol Records, who advised him to drop the James Loden, and adopt the professional stage name *Sonny James*.

James' first chart hit for Capitol was "That's Me Without You," a 1953 Top Ten single. The following year, he charted a number fourteen single, which he wrote: "She Done Give Her Heart To Me." There was a dry spell, until his co-write "For Rent (One Empty Heart)" brought him back into the country Top Ten in 1956, but later that year came "Young Love," a romantic lament for which he'll always be remembered. That 45-rpm single topped both the pop and country charts in early 1957, spending an impressive nine weeks at number one country.

Sonny James jacket to his 1981 single 'Innocent Lies.

In chartings, James recorded sixteen number one country singles in a row, a record at the time, and boasted a grand total of twenty-six chart-toppers, among seventy-two chartings over a thirty-year period (1953-'83).

It was in 1957 that James married Doris Shrode in Dallas, Texas. She admired his great sense of humor, and smiled in remembering the "trick" fiddle he used for a time as part of his act. He'd say, "Now we're going to do a fiddle tune," but when he started playing it, the fiddle fell apart. Actually, he was as fine a fiddler, as he was guitarist and singer, and in 1973, donned a new hat, becoming a record producer. Sonny guided young Marie Osmond to her first number one single, "Paper Roses," a multi-million seller, and an equally successful debut album.

In 1977, Sonny James recorded an album in the Tennessee State Prison, "In Prison, In Person," backed by a band of inmates. Your author worked for Sonny and Doris independently for a time, administering their publishing company and doing his session contracts: "Sonny was the kindest person I ever met in over sixty years in the music business."

Ruth White's friend Don Davis agreed, noting that when he produced Connie Cato for Capitol Records, they were recording the tune "Here Comes That Rainy Day Feeling Again," and he wanted "a Sonny James sound" on guitar. Well, Don called Sonny to ask if he could guide them. When Davis arrived at the studio the next day, there was James with guitar in hand. That single charted in 1976, and a grateful Davis said, "There's no one as generous as Sonny James."

So we know why they tagged him the "The Southern Gentleman." He has also earned his share of accolades: In 1961, Sonny was the first country artist honored with a star on Hollywood's Walk of Fame; in 1962, he was added to WSM's *Grand Ole Opry* cast; in 1987, he was voted into the Alabama Music Hall of Fame; awarded a Golden Voice Award in 2001; honored with a 2002 Career Achievement Award by the Country DJ Hall of Fame; and inducted into the Country Music Hall of Fame in 2006.

Sonny James' voice was stilled on February 22, 2016, when he died at age eighty-seven.

19 JAM-UP & HONEY ...
Tent Show Specialists

Lee Davis (Honey) Wilds and Leroy Robert (Lasses) White were black-face comedians, who worked on WNOX's *The Mid-Day Merry-Go-Round*, and regarded as the local station's answer to NBC radio's nationally-famous duo *Amos 'n' Andy*. Their comedy act was a quarter-hour "soap opera" in black-face.

In 1932, White and Wilds took their act to WSM's Opry, initially billed as "Lasses White's Minstrels," and also proved popular in personal appearances with the cast. When White left the act, to make movies in Hollywood, Wilds first added Tom Woods briefly, then Bunny Biggs, and after that, Harry LeVan to the act, now being called JamUp & Honey.

Reportedly, they created the Opry Tent Shows, which also featured such stars as Roy Acuff, Hank Williams, Ernest Tubb and the Poe Sisters on the bill. Once on a tent show, Pee Wee King & His Golden West Cowboys were headlining. King musicians' Grady Martin and Don Davis were the troupe's unofficial pranksters. They found a dead King Snake about five feet long and decided to play a joke on JamUp & Honey. They got a string and tied it around the snake's neck and put it on one side of the stage. Then they pulled the string, dragging the snake across the stage.

JamUp & Honey

Waiting until JamUp & Honey were in the middle of their routine, they started pulling that snake across and as they maneuvered the snake in front of them, JamUp & Honey looked down and the excitement began. Honey left the stage, and no one knew if he went left, right, or front of the stage. He just disappeared. JamUp backed away from the snake, but being the pro that he was, continued on with the act, though it took quite a while to find Honey.

JamUp & Honey was a hard act to beat. They imitated famous people, performing in black-face or "burnt cork" as they called it then. Honey once acted out a "sunburnt Arthur Godfrey," a popular TV host, while JamUp specialized in "Bert Williams' type comedy." As times changed, JamUp &

Honey became the last of the minstrel acts on the WSM *Opry,* for such shows were being deemed racially offensive.

Lasses White died at age sixty-one, shortly after filming a Western "The Texan Meets Calamity Jane" with Evelyn Ankers, in 1949; Bunny Biggs died August 28, 1948, at age fifty-one; and Lee Davis Wilds died on March 29, 1982, at age seventy-nine.

20 PEE WEE KING...
Golden West Cowboy

"My memory leads back
To a tumble down shack
Down by the lonesome pine
I'm leaving today heading that way
To that old fashioned mother of mine."

Early King song by Joe L. Frank

Pee Wee King was born February 18, 1914 to a working class family in Milwaukee, Wisconsin. Christened Julius Frank Anthony Kuczynski, his parents were first-generation Americans, though all his grandparents came from Europe: three from Poland and one from Austria. Polish was spoken at home and "Pee Wee" grew up playing polkas on the accordion.

Pee Wee formed his first band in high school, Frankie King & The King's Jesters, borrowing the name from pop music's famed "Waltz King," Wayne King. Gene Autry hired them as a backup band at WLS-Chicago and was the one who gave him the nickname *Pee Wee*.

King liked Autry's new name for him, and had it changed to Frank Pee Wee King. He landed his own radio show on WJRN-Racine, Wisconsin. Texan Gene Autry helped give Pee Wee a sense of what to do musically, but when Joe L. Frank became his manager, Joe showed him how to do it best. Frank was a natural-born promoter, who brought Pee Wee into Frankie More's band The Log Cabin Boys in Louisville, Kentucky. They put WHAS-Louisville on the air every morning, and came back at one p.m.

They did the big Saturday night show, *Crazy Water Barn Dance*, sponsored of course by Crazy Water Crystals. Louisville was an ideal spot in the 1930s for country acts. Pee Wee and band were happy there, but Frank got a phone call from Joe Pearson, WNOX station manager, in Knoxville. He said, "There's room here for a guy like Pee Wee King, and The Log Cabin Boys. I've got the perfect set-up for y'all. Come on down."

It was perfect timing, for The Log Cabin Boys were breaking up. Nobody, including Mr. Frank, was making any money. WNOX offered them a hundred dollars a week, divided among seven people. But, that seemed like a lot of money in 1935, so they accepted the offer, and it provided them with a small, but steady income.

When Pee Wee arrived at the new studios of WNOX, he was shocked. The walls, furniture and curtains were all done in different shades of black. When the lights came on, it looked like a funeral parlor. Pee Wee complained, but Mr. Frank only said, "It's worth a try." Pee Wee and the Log Cabin Boys immediately began on the *Mid-Day Merry-Go-Round*. There were a lot of different acts, including Roy Acuff, Archie Campbell, Cliff and Bill Carlisle, Homer & Jethro, and a four-piece band called Albany Musco & His Modern Band. Lowell Blanchard was announcing.

Pee Wee and the Log Cabin Boys did at least one number a day, hoping to make it a signature song, which people might remember them by. Radio listeners used to try and guess what the performers looked like. Archie teased Pee Wee saying, "Pee Wee, do people mistake you for someone else?" Pee Wee said, "Yeah, they think I'm a big heavy-set guy named Tiny, who used to work on *The Barn Dance.*"

The benches in the broadcast studio were filled every day. Most of them were town-folk who came in for the free show on lunch break, along with a few people from the farms, who slipped away from their fields for an hour. Radio listeners consisted of people out in the country, who came into the house from their plowing at dinner time to tune in. On Saturday nights, the troupe played the *Tennessee Barn Dance,* which did a three-hour show, and the studio would be mostly overflowing.

Other nights they worked at nearby venues and advertised their radio connection. Regardless of where they played, they knew they had to be back for the daily and Saturday night shows. At WNOX, they got paid their regular salary. What they made on the road was extra.

When Pee Wee was twenty-two, he and Mr. Frank's nineteen-year-old stepdaughter Lydia, ran off to Sevierville, twenty-five miles east of Knoxville, and got married. (Lydia's real dad was musician August Winkler, who died when she was three.) Pee Wee and Lydia's marriage lasted a life-time.

Joe L., Pee Wee and The Log Cabin Boys stayed at WNOX through all of 1936. Near the end of their stay, Mr. Frank decided to disband The Log Cabin Boys. Pee Wee then formed his Golden West Cowboys, borrowing the title from a WLS trio, Girls Of The Golden West. But they decided to go back to Louisville, and debut the new band. They were happy to be returning to Kentucky, after deciding they had burned out the Knoxville territory.

In November 1936, however, just before leaving WNOX, the station exercised an option and extended their contract for eight weeks. So they played out the option before moving back to Louisville. Their grand band debut coincided with the biggest flood ever seen in Louisville. Subsequently, they spent eleven days huddled together with little food, no lights or heat. After that, they were fortunate to be booked for thirty-three days at a local theater.

Pee Wee had no plans for Nashville, as most other artists did upon leaving Knoxville. But, right on the heels of the Louisville disaster, they got an invitation in 1937, to appear on WSM's *Grand Ole Opry.* By then, they were a well-rehearsed, versatile band, complete with an Opry sponsor, Royal Crown Cola. At the time, the Opry paid nothing, and you worked for the advertising of your shows.

In 1940, Pee Wee King and his Golden West Cowboys moved back to the town Pee Wee loved, Louisville, at WAVE radio. Among his lead vocalists, who went on to solo stardom, were Eddy Arnold and Cowboy Copas. In 1947, Pee Wee pioneered a popular WAVE-TV variety show in Louisville.

With Redd Stewart, Pee Wee co-wrote classic country songs, some of which crossed over into the pop charts, notably "The Tennessee Waltz," "Slow Poke," "You Belong To Me" and an instrumental success "Bonaparte's Retreat." Pee Wee had a hit twice on his recording of "Tennessee Waltz"

(1948 and 1951), as well as hit singles with "Tennessee Polka," "Tennessee Tears," and further Top Tens with "Silver and Gold," "Busybody," "Changing Partners" and "Bimbo." His sole number one, "Slow Poke," a multi-million seller, was in top spot fifteen weeks of its thirty-one weeks' charting.

He hosted *The Pee Wee King Show* on ABC-TV six years, appeared in Western films, including Gene Autry's "Gold Mine In The Sky," Johnny Mack Brown's "Flame Of The West" and Charles (Durango Kid) Starrett's "Ridin' The Outlaw Trail." Numerous other artists also recorded his songs, notably Patti Page, Cowboy Copas, Jo Stafford, Guy Lombardo, Les Paul & Mary Ford, Kay Starr and Glen Campbell.

In 1969, Pee Wee disbanded the Golden West Cowboys, having kept the band together in one form or another, more than thirty years. He occasionally worked as a single, but began to slow down in the 1970s and '80s. In 1974, Pee Wee became a member of the Country Music Hall of Fame, as had his father-in-law Joe L. Frank (1967).

Except for *Merry-Go-Round* reunions, Pee Wee would never again perform in Knoxville. The last reunion was held September 13, 1992 at David's *Music Barn,* six miles north of Knoxville, but by then there weren't many old-timers left. He died March 7, 2000, at age eighty-six, perhaps remembering his biggest money-making tune, "The Tennessee Waltz," an official state song.

"I remember the night, and the Tennessee Waltz
Now I know just how much I have lost,
Yes, I lost my little darlin',
The night they were playing
The beautiful Tennessee Waltz . . ."

Pee Wee King-Redd Stewart

Here's a vintage shot of the Golden West Cowboys plugging Royal Crown Cola,
and in the front row are (from left) Redd Stewart, Becky Barfield, Shorty Reed,
Pee Wee King and Don Davis, circa 1947.

21 THE LOUVIN BROTHERS...
Ira and Charlie Loudermilk

The Louvin Brothers were a legendary music duo comprised of Ira Lonnie Loudermilk and Charlie Elzer Loudermilk, better known as Ira and Charlie Louvin. The boys were first cousins to future hit songwriter John D. Loudermilk. They adopted their stage name Louvin in 1947, while working at WROL-Knoxville, seeking an easier name for fans to remember.

The brothers born in Henagar, Alabama, grew up picking cotton, hunting with "Papa" and singing songs with "Mama," the daughter of a Baptist preacher. With their Papa playing on a claw-hammer banjo, music became Ira and Charlie's pastime and ultimately their passion.

At their Sacred Harp Church, the siblings first experimented with what would later become their trademark harmonies. Music became their escape from life in the cottonfields. They earned their first fifty dollars for playing all day on a mule-drawn merry-go-round at a July 4th celebration.

As teenagers they became the 4:30 a.m. regulars on WDEF-Chattanooga, after winning a talent contest. Ira played mandolin like Bill Monroe and sang in an impossibly high quivering tenor, while Charlie strummed guitar, sang the lower harmony and was always grinning. They made close-harmony vocals popular on stage. After WDEF, the Louvins went to WNOX's *Mid-Day-Merry-Go-Round* and *Tennessee Barn Dance*. On WNOX's daytime show, they performed with Hack and Clyde Johnson.

Ira was a cut-up, acting as *Sal Skinner* in drag, for a routine with Lowell Blanchard. The premise of Sal Skinner was that she was from Financial Flats, Tennessee. It was a hyped-up, frenzied Minnie Pearl-type, with Ira playing Sal, garbed in a bonnet and old-fashioned gingham dress.

By 1946, the Louvins had moved to WMPS-Memphis, joined by Eddie Hill, for a noon-day show. The Louvin Brothers harmony style came naturally as did their superb songwriting. Charlie claimed he was the idea man, but Ira took Charlie's ideas and made them into a song without any effort.

The duo landed a Capitol Records contract, but performed primarily gospel. In 1955, however, they were allowed to record their own secular creation, "When I Stop Dreaming," giving them their first Top Ten single. That same year, Ira and Charlie joined *The Grand Ole Opry*.

It was shortly afterwards their troubles began. Ira's heavy drinking and temper tantrums disabled their shows. The irascible older brother became infamous for smashing his mandolin on stage when he couldn't tune it to his satisfaction. When sober, Ira would put it back together again, having the ability to carve and create anything out of wood. He once carved a whole manger scene, from the Wise Men to Baby Jesus.

Ira once told Elvis Presley he thought his music was crap, while on tour together. Due to all the drinking, Ira started going downhill and it got so the brothers were only in harmony when singing. After years of quarreling, it all came to a head one night at a party in 1963 at Ira and third

Ira & Charlie Louvin on the Opry.

wife Fay's home. Ira, Fay, Ira's sisters, Roy Acuff and Shot Jackson were all there. Reportedly, a lot of whiskey was consumed.

This writer and husband Howard White were in the house the next day at the request of Fay's brother, Johnny Johnson. Johnny wanted us to help clean up. We saw two waste baskets full of empty whiskey bottles. Acuff said he and Jackson had gone to get more whiskey and were not there when all hell broke loose. Fay put six bullets into Ira, but he lived. She said he was choking her with the phone cord. It was apparent a fight had gone on, after viewing the house the next day.

Soon after, WSM Opry Manager Ott Devine called Charlie into his office and told him he could stay on at the Opry, but Ira could not: Ira was fired! That finished The Louvin Brothers act, and Charlie stayed on the Opry and began recording solo successes such as "I Don't Love You Anymore" and "See The Big Man Cry." The Louvin Brothers' final chart record was "Must You Throw Dirt In My Face," a 1962 Top Twenty single. Ira also recorded solo, but with less success, the best being his posthumous Top Forty charting, "Yodel, Sweet Molly," in August 1965.

Throughout the years, the story was that Ira's drinking was the reason for the breakup, and certainly was an indirect cause, but your author was working for Ott Devine at WSM when he held his private meeting with Charlie, issuing management's ultimatum and firing Ira in 1963. It was the straw that broke the camel's back so to speak. Incidentally, despite the gun play, Fay and Ira reconciled for a short time, but then divorced.

Sadly, Ira died in a head-on collision with his fourth wife, Anne, June 20, 1965, while returning home after a show. He was forty-one years old. The Louvin Brothers, who influenced such latter-day stars as Emmylou Harris, were inducted into the Country Music Hall of Fame in 2001. Charlie remained an Opry star until his death on January 26, 2011, at age eighty-three.

"When I Stop Dreaming,
I'll still be in love with you."

Ira & Charlie Louvin

22 MOLLY O'DAY . . .
'Mountain Fern'

> *"Some mother rocked him, Her darlin' to sleep*
> *But they left him to die, Like a tramp on the street."*
>
> Hazel & Grady Cole.

Lois Laverne Williamson, better known as Molly O'Day, was born on July 9, 1923 in Paintsville, Kentucky, the daughter of a coal-miner. Her mournful singing had a major impact on country music and especially music icon Fred Rose. Some historians called her the "female Hank Williams," and Molly was the first notable artist to record Hank's songs, which included "Six More Miles To the Graveyard" and "The Singing Waterfall."

When Laverne's brother Cecil (Skeets) Williamson landed a job on a Charleston, West Virginia radio station in 1939, he sent for his sweet-voiced sixteen-year-old sister, dubbed her "Mountain Fern" and featured her on the air with him.

Later she also adopted the stage name "Dixie Lee" Williamson. She and her brothers Skeets and Joe worked with Johnnie Bailes' Happy Valley Boys, before joining Leonard (Lynn) Davis and his band The Forty-Niners in Bluefield, West Virginia.

In April 1941, Laverne married Lynn Davis, and their life became a series of moves from radio station to radio station in states such as Alabama and Kentucky. While at WHAS-Louisville, she took the name "Molly O'Day." Molly was no slouch as a banjo player, pickin' with a drop-thumb style. Once, she even beat Earl Scruggs in a Renfro Valley Pickin' Contest. She had a great ear for fresh material, but also had a fascination with cowgirl songs of the previous generation, like Patsy Montana. Her "Banjo Pickin' Girl" became the anthem for all free-spirited country music women with a yen to ramble.

Art Satherley produces Molly O'Day's 1946 Chicago session, with musicians Mac Wiseman and Lynn Davis.

Molly and her husband moved to Knoxville in 1945, to WNOX's *Mid-Day Merry-Go-Round* and *The Tennessee Barn Dance*. This is where she achieved her greatest popularity, selling song books and mailing fan photos as fast as they could be printed.

Leslie Keith, who wrote "Black Mountain Rag," put Mac Wiseman wise to the fact that Molly and Lynn had an opening in their Cumberland

Mountain Folks group. Keith also told the group, "I know who you need, Mac Wiseman." Then Lynn sent Mac a telegram, telling him to come to WNOX and audition. They hired Mac right away in the Fall of 1946. Mac began opening shows for Molly, as warm-up acts do today. He'd sing for fifteen or twenty minutes, performing whatever was currently popular at the time, then bring on the show's star attraction, Miss Molly.

The first thing the band would do when they got to a venue, was move the chairs as close to the stage as they could, because they were going to need standing room. They did two or three shows a night, for that's how popular Molly O'Day was. Mainly, they played a lot of school houses up in the mountain region and throughout rural areas.

Mac remembered one time they pulled up as close to a school as they could, because they had to cross a small drawbridge on a narrow path that wound around the mountain. They saw the school lights were on, and had a bulky sound system, too heavy for one man to carry, so Mac and Skeets carried it together. Mac, who had a bad polio leg, and Skeets struggled to lug it up the mountainside. When they got up to the school, they found those "lights" they saw were only kerosene lamps. There was no electricity! Mac and Skeets didn't know whether to laugh or cry.

Songwriter-publisher Fred Rose became an O'Day champion, and convinced Columbia's A&R chief Arthur (Uncle Art) Satherley to sign and record her. Art had Molly and her band report to WBBM radio station in Chicago, at 410 North Michigan Avenue, to record her first session. Reportedly, they recorded "Tramp On The Street," "When God Comes And Gathers His Jewels," "The Black Sheep Returned To The Fold," and "Put My Rubber Doll Away." Additionally, they also cut four Acuff-Rose copyrights: "The Tear-Stained Letter," "Drunken Driver," "Six More Miles To The Graveyard" and "Lonely Mound Of Clay." On the session with Molly were Skeets, fiddle; Mac, bass; George (Speedy) Krise, Dobro; and Lynn on guitar. The recordings boasted Molly's emotional lead vocals, as she played guitar or banjo. Molly was one of the few women that Uncle Art recorded country, and he had high hopes for her commercial success.

Molly O'Day was a pivotol country music figure, singing in an openly emotional, mournful mountain manner that stirred the heart. She sang with Appalachian fervor, creating a throbbing, chilling delivery that influenced women vocalists for years. Art Satherley called her the greatest female country singer of all time, and even Earl Scruggs respected her banjo playing talent.

In the midst of her popularity, Molly began to question her entertainment life and turned to recording more religious music. In 1949, she suffered a nervous breakdown. Three months later, she and husband Lynn joined The First Church Of God. Molly left Acuff-Rose and recorded her last recordings for Columbia in 1950 and '51. Between 1946-1951, she recorded thirty-six songs for Columbia, but never attained the success that Satherley and Rose had envisioned for her.

It was in 1954 that Lynn became an ordained minister, then he and Molly gave up their careers to serve The First Church Of God. At this point, she sang gospel exclusively, notably "Matthew Twenty-Four." She had been with WNOX five years, and passed on becoming a female country star by devoting her life to Evangelism, despite memorable successes such as "Poor Ellen Smith" and "Teardrops Falling In The Snow."

On Old Homestead Records, there's "Molly O'Day and The Cumberland Mountain Folks: A Sacred Collection," featuring the single "Don't Sell Daddy Any More Whiskey," complete with a baby crying in the background all the way through the track (a wee bit distracting to some ears).

Producer Robert Mooney was the last to record Molly on his REM Records album: "Molly O'Day Sings Again." To record her, Mooney went twenty-five miles up a "holler" to a little old church house. According to Mooney, "The congregation had a lot of devoted people, who shouted the Lord's praises until red in the face." REM, one of the smallest labels specializing in country music, operated out of a shack behind the Lexington, Kentucky home of Mooney (a former employee of King Records). Mooney started REM in 1960, to "record real country music," and sold records out of his car. Molly had left the music business for service with the First Church Of God in Huntington, West Virginia, when Mooney recorded her. But she and Lynn hosted a gospel radio program *Hymns From The Hills* in1973, broadcast by WEMM-Huntington.

Molly used to joke that she was from so far back in a Kentucky hollow that they had to break daylight with a sledge hammer. Molly O'Day died of cancer on December 4, 1987 at age 64, in Huntington. In her last days, Molly opined, "I sing from the heart. I always have. I don't think they're doing that these days." O'Day is credited with pioneering the role of the solo female country artist.

23 CARL SMITH . . .

"I overlooked an orchid,
While searching for a rose,
The orchid that I overlooked was you,
The rose that I was searching for
Has proved to be untrue,
And the orchid now I find my dear was you . . ."

Carl Smith, Carl Story, Shirley Lyn (Troy Martin)

Carl Milton Smith was born March 15, 1927 on a farm near Maynard-ville, Tennessee. As a youngster he listened to WNOX and WROL beaming from Knoxville. While a school boy, his parents bought him a guitar, and Carl mowed lawns to pay for guitar lessons.

At thirteen, he first sang on the radio, participating in an amateur talent program. After that, he was determined to be a singer and while in high school, convinced Cas Walker to let him sing on WROL-Knoxville, which included playing a bass, not his usual instrument.

That was all interrupted when he was called to active duty in the Navy in 1944, just three days before his scheduled graduation. He spent eleven of eighteen months' sea duty on a ship sailing the Pacific. Following discharge, Carl landed radio spots singing in Augusta, Georgia, and Asheville, North Carolina.

Smith was pleased by an offer to join WNOX's *Mid-Day Merry-Go-Round* and *The Tennessee Barn Dance*, bringing him back to his hometown. Like another of his cast mates, Carl was a prankster, pulling a slick one on Bill Carlisle a.k.a. Hotshot Elmer. That occurred while playing straight man for Carlisle's comedy routine, which had Bill portraying a drunk with the DT's, whose only "fix" was a shot of whiskey. Carl was supposed to put Coca Cola in a whiskey bottle and rush a shot on stage to Bill at the mic; this time, however, abetted by cast-mates Ira and Charlie Louvin, he actually slipped a very bad cheap whiskey into Bill's bottle. Of course, Bill swallowed it fast, before realizing it wasn't a Coke, and then Carl poured him another quick shot, but by then Carlisle was on to him, ad-libbing, "Boy, I sure do dread this next 'fix'!"

Oddly enough, newly-signed Carl recorded a hit song for Columbia Records in July 1950, that didn't register with *Billboard*, titled "I Overlooked An Orchid," which he, Carl Story and Troy Martin had bought from Arthur Q. Smith (no relation). Steel player Billy Robinson remembers when he cut that session with Carl, with Grady Martin on guitar and Ernie Newton playing bass. Although it brought Carl to the attention of audiences across America, it didn't chart, due to the trade magazine's short country listing, sometimes even reduced to less than ten, dependent on space available.

84

Carl's growing popularity was enhanced by his movie star good looks, including piercing blue eyes, wavy dark hair, and slim six-foot, two-inch torso. Teen-agers and matrons alike squealed with delight on seeing and hearing the Maynardville flash! Hank Williams, Jr., recalls Carl's affect even in later years, "I was a boy, but I remember that guy was real striking to the ladies. I remember that reaction when he went out on stage."

It was also in 1950, that Carl successfully auditioned for program director Jack Stapp at WSM. When Carl started out at the station, he said he played three days a week, Monday, Wednesday and Friday with a band at 6:15 a.m.; then it was 5:15 a.m. on Tuesday, Thursday and Saturday. On Sunday morning, Carl did a fifteen-minute hymn program, no band, just him and his guitar: "They wouldn't let me have one picker. An announcer put me on and then disappeared."

Carl has said that's where he got the greatest education, because in radio you have to visualize the people out there listening. Even in Nashville, Carl was still a master prankster. Early in his Nashville days, he lived at Mom Upchurch's Boarding House. If musicians living there had a car, when they went on the road, a musician without a car could borrow his car while he was gone. Dale Potter, a fiddler, liked to tell the story about steel player Frankie Kay. Frankie was dating June Carter and whenever he left town, he would leave his car at June's house. One

GI Mel Fristadt meets his hero Carl Smith.

day, Dale asked Frankie, "Hey, does Carl Smith like your car?" Of course, Dale knew Carl was spending time with June when Frankie was out of town. Dale just wanted to instigate some trouble, and that was how Frankie discovered Carl was borrowing his car . . . and his girl.

In fact, Carl married June Carter in 1952. They became the hot, young "royal" couple of country music, complete with duets in 1953, "Love, Oh Crazy Love" and "Time's A'Wastin'." They had one daughter, Rebecca Carlene Smith, in 1955. Later, she became a singer, choosing the name Carlene Carter. Carl and June divorced in 1956, and in 1957 Carl married singer Goldie Hill. (June remarried twice, once to Rip Nix in 1960 and then Johnny Cash in 1968.)

Nashville-based talent scout Troy Martin had a hand in promoting Carl Smith's career. He worked awhile for Peer-Southern music publishers, and brought them some of their richest copyrights, including Lefty Frizzell's "If You Got The Money, I Got The Time" and "I Love You A Thousand Ways," Kitty Wells' "It Wasn't God Who Made Honky Tonk Angels" and Carl & Pearl Butler's "Don't Let Me Cross Over." What the publisher didn't know was occasionally their scout was drawing extra pay by buying into songs such as "I Overlooked An Orchid," substituting the name Shirley Lyn (his wife's name) onto the copyright.

While Jim Denny was General Manager and head of Artists Service Bureau at WSM, he started a publishing company with Carl Smith and Webb Pierce as partners in 1953. Together they founded Cedarwood and Driftwood Music Publishing. Then in 1956, Jack DeWitt aware of the potential conflict of interest decided to ban moonlighting at WSM. But Denny would not give up his lucrative publishing interests, so he was fired. This action prompted Carl and Webb to leave the Opry, as well. Carl began working regularly on television, most notably Springfield, Missouri's *Ozark Jubilee* ABC telecasts. Meantime, Cedarwood struck gold when Webb Pierce hit big with "Slowly," number one seventeen of its thirty-six weeks *Billboard* charting. Smith, too, continued to turn out the hits, including "Hey Joe," "Loose Talk," "Back Up Buddy" and "Ten Thousand Drums."

Although from Acuff's hometown Maynardville, Smith brought a different sound to his hits, blending in a more modern Western Swing feel to songs like "Go Boy Go," while still delivering warmth and feeling into romantic ballads, such as "Let Old Mother Nature Have Her Way" and "Don't Just Stand There." Even in the 1960s, he produced successes such as "Deep Water" and continued to record into the 1970s, accumulating ninety-three chart songs before retiring from music in 1978.

Carl himself was far from retiring, for he bred champion cutting horse for decades out there on his five hundred-acre ranch in Franklin, just down the highway from Nashville. Asked about his second career, Carl acknowledged: "I just wanted to play cowboy. My philosophy is doing what I want to do."

In 2003, rather belatedly, Carl Smith was inducted into the Country Music Hall Of Fame, but Carl's reaction was simple, "I appreciate it very much. I thought they wouldn't put me in until I died." A friend Merle Kilgore, himself a singer-songwriter, mused, "People forgot about Carl Smith, when he stopped singing and stepped out of the limelight. (But) he made money and invested it wisely." Hank Williams, Jr., told Carl upon his induction: "That took awhile didn't it? Something went right today." Outlaw Waylon Jennings didn't attend his own Country Music Hall Of Fame award night, noting he would not go into any Hall Of Fame that didn't include Carl Smith. So, Carl may have been forgotten for a time, by those in power, but his artist friends loved him and remembered. Carl's friends all thought it strange that Carl never got to say a word on the air during the CMA awards telecast. "What gives?," they asked. They knew though that Carl was not the type to complain. Carl's wife Goldie, however, acknowledged: "What made up for it, was the standing ovation that lasted and lasted."

Truth is Carl was prepared to make remarks, and while backstage was thinking about his statement, until someone from production came by to tell him he wasn't going to be allowed to say anything on camera, so he could go sit in the audience with his wife. Later, the show's producer said it was all a misunderstanding, that they had been told Carl didn't want to speak on camera, so instead they allotted time "to focus on his wonderful standing ovation."

Masterful hanky-tonk singer and dashing country gentleman, Carl Smith, died on his beloved ranch January 16, 2010, at age eighty-two. His wife, Goldie Hill Smith, had died previously on February 24, 2005, at age seventy-two. Let's always remember that this talented man from Maynard-ville, knew what he wanted from boyhood on, and did it, living life exactly as he wanted.

24 KITTY WELLS AND JOHNNIE & JACK...

"'Cause we stuck together through the lean, lean years
The lean and hungry years were filled with strife
Now we're still together in the green, green years
And we'll stick together for the rest of our life . . . "

Bill Phillips

Ellen Muriel Deason was born August 30, 1919 in Nashville, Tennessee. Her family lived on Wharf Avenue in the city's south side. "Baby Muriel" had Irish and American Indian blood in her veins. Her father played guitar, and Kitty remembered from ages three and four that she used to sit on the floor, listening to her father and family, singing the old songs. Their "family sing" also included gospel songs. As she grew up, and became a teen-ager, her singing and playing began to impress people. Her father was so pleased, he gave her his guitar and never played it again.

Johnnie Robert Wright was born May 13, 1914 in Mt. Juliet, just down the pike from Nashville.

Muriel met Johnnie when she was sixteen years old in 1935. Johnnie's sister, Bessie, lived next door to the Deasons. He visited Bessie one day, and while Johnnie was playing guitar, Bessie sent for Muriel to come over to sing and play with them. Soon after, he and Muriel began dating, and before long their friendship developed into love. Johnnie asked Muriel to marry him, and they wed on Halloween eve 1937, after she had turned eighteen.

Earlier, Muriel and her cousin Bessie Choate had also started singing together, calling themselves The Deason Sisters. At that time, twenty-five hundred-watt WSIX-Nashville was broadcasting country music in the area and had an "open mike" program Saturdays, *The Old Country Store.* Anyone who had some singing ability could try out. In 1935, the Deason Sisters auditioned and WSIX liked them, and gave them a fifteen-minute program at 6:15 a.m. When Bessie took sick, Johnnie and his sister Louise joined Muriel (in 1936). Suddenly their WSIX billing became *Johnnie Wright & His Harmony Girls.*

Meanwhile, Johnnie had met the Anglin brothers, Jack, Jim and Van (Red), who appeared on WSIX, as well. When a brother didn't show, Johnnie would fill in. Jim and Van really didn't cotton to performing, so soon Jack teamed with Johnnie, playing local shows. Besides their love of music, the two shared the same birthday - May 13 - though Johnnie was two years senior, and Jack was the same age as Louise, whom he would marry (June 1938). All of them had day jobs, mainly working nights and weekends as musicians, with Johnnie and Jack admittedly inspired by the Delmore Brothers.

88

A catastrophe that brought Johnnie and Jack together as a team, occurred when the rampaging Ohio River flooded communities in a tri-state area in early 1937, bringing death and devastation to those in its path. That prompted the new duo to perform and help raise flood relief funds, traveling as far north as Cincinnati. As The Backwater Boys, Johnnie sang lead, and Jack usually sang tenor.

In 1939, Johnnie, Jack, and local musicians, Paul Warren, Emory Martin and Ernie Ferguson, became The Roving Cowboys on WSIX-Nashville, but soon evolved as The Tennessee Hillbillies, occasionally featuring guest vocals by Muriel and Louise. The "Cowboys" had to get up before dawn to get to the station, situated in the old Andrew Jackson Hotel, by 5 o'clock, then rush off to day jobs.

Promoter George Peek heard them on the radio, and asked if the troupe had considered working away from Nashville, as he had contacts, specifically at WBIG-Greensboro, North Carolina. That was a hard decision for Johnnie and Jack, who by now had wives to think about, and Muriel and Johnnie had their first child, Ruby Jean, born October 27, 1939.

Right after the Christmas holidays in 1940, Peek had convinced the band to take the opening at WBIG, so Johnnie gave up his carpentry job at Davis Cabinet Company, Jack did the same at Selig Hosiery, and Muriel at Washington Manufacturing, to make their move. It was a risky

Candid shot of Tennessee Mountain Boys Johnnie Wright, (daughter Carol Sue, wife Kitty Wells), Shot Jackson and Jack Anglin in Cincinnati, Ohio.

decision, as the WBIG offer came without contract or up-front money or salary, and no guarantees.

Surprisingly, things went well for awhile, as Wright hustled up a furniture store sponsor, and their show landed them bookings throughout the area. That is, until Charlie Monroe (Bill's brother), a bigger WBIG act grew envious of their growing popularity, and complained to station management. He said Johnnie & Jack sang too much like the Monroe Brothers, and their blackface comedy routine with Johnnie as Petunia and Paul as Butterbean, was too similar to Charlie's comic Stringbean (David Akeman). Aware of the ultimatum management was facing, Johnnie went to Charlie, telling him they didn't mean to hurt Monroe's show, they only wanted to try and make a living. All Charlie could say was "You got Butterbean and I got Stringbean, one of us has to go."

Peek was peeved, but was able to get WCHS-Charleston, West Virginia, interested in his act. It was a fifty-thousand watt station, and Johnnie, Jack and their crew appeared on *The Old Farm Hour.* Crowds packed the station's eight-hundred-seat auditorium to see them. Part of their act featured Emory Martin, a one-armed banjo player, playing with his feet and even his teeth. He played with the banjo neck lying across his left knee, noting it with his stub of an arm, and pickin' with his good right hand. Also playing was Paul Warren, a fiddle player, who credited Wright for giving him his first professional break as a musician and comedian, before working with Flatt & Scruggs and Roy Acuff; and Ernie Ferguson, mandolin, who later played for the Bailes Brothers and a young Roy Clark.

They traveled to nearby venues in Johnnie's 1937 Chevy. Their instruments were put in the trunk and carried their big bass fiddle on top of the car, unless it was raining. Then it was put inside, with all of them crowding around, it along with a P.A. system.

Doing well in West Virginia, they had the feeling good times were just ahead, Then a bid came in from WNOX Knoxville, as Lowell Blanchard invited them on the *Mid-Day Merry-Go-Round.* It was in June 1942 they left Charleston for Knoxville. Soon, new mom Muriel (she had given birth to son Bobby in March) started becoming very popular with WNOX listeners, no doubt thanks to that little tremor in her vocals. Sincerity is the word to best describe her no-frills singing. They were also playing the station's *Tennessee Barn Dance* on the weekend.

Lowell Blanchard decided that Muriel might be too hard a name for folks to remember, telling Johnnie: "If you change her name, she could make a hit out there." Johnnie remembered a ballad he knew from childhood called "Sweet Kitty Wells," and suggested that to Blanchard, who liked that idea. From that point on, the former Muriel Deason became *Kitty Wells.*

After America plunged into World War II, with the Japanese bombing of Pearl Harbor in Hawaii, everybody's life was affected in one way or another. The Draft called up younger musicians, and gas rationing also hurt show people, who depended on working the road to make ends meet. Jack Anglin was drafted into the Army, and Johnnie and company's gas ration card only allowed them three gallons a week, putting an end to their road shows.

Kitty and Johnnie and their crew returned to Nashville. Wright went to work at DuPont Chemical Company, and Kitty became a homemaker again. "Smiling" Eddie Hill, like Johnnie, had show business in his blood. Eddie would wear many hats, including that of musician, singer-songwriter, and emcee. He had a flair for pleasing an audience and later became a popular DJ.

Well, Eddie and Johnnie got together and decided to regroup a band, using Johnnie's extra gas rations due to working for a war plant like DuPont, and hit the road again, doing shows. Kitty was also a key part of the act, and Lowell Blanchard let it be known he would welcome them back to Knoxville.

For this return to the *Mid-Day Merry-Go-Round* and *Tennessee Barn Dance*, Johnnie added a comedy act with Eddie as Hump Hammer and Johnnie portraying Cousin Nimrod, who was introduced on stage as "the old maid's heartthrob." While they all did well, Kitty's heartfelt singing drew more mail than any other member. Johnnie was delighted and arranged for new publicity pictures for his whole group. Kitty's pose called for a vintage costume, consisting of floor-length peasant dress and sunbonnet to frame her dark hair. Of course, Johnnie and Eddie also posed as hayseed comics Cousin Nimrod and Hump Hammer.

It was in Knoxville that they hired young Chet Atkins to become a Tennessee Hillbilly, but this time he was engaged as a fiddler. Johnnie even issued a songbook with their pictures, biographies and song lyrics, which they "hawked" on the air and at road shows. Reportedly, they sold in excess of one hundred thousand booklets. In addition to their other WNOX programs, they also did an early morning broadcast aimed at the farmers and other early risers.

Traveling country roads of the 1940s was not easy and sometimes proved dangerous, especially riding in Eddie Hill's souped-up 1941 Oldsmobile, nicknamed "The Torpedo." Once on a four-lane highway out of Knoxville, Eddie really opened it up, causing Kitty in the backseat to cry out, "Slow down! Slow down!"

One night, Eddie was speeding and when Kitty cautioned him to slow down again, he said he had to outrun a state trooper in Kentucky, because he didn't have money for a fine. When the speedometer hit ninety miles an hour, he hit the brake to slow down after Kitty yelled, "Slow down or let me out!"

On another occasion after leaving a show date, Eddie flipped the car over twice, landing right side up. Kitty and Johnnie in the backseat weren't hurt, but Eddie got grease on his head and mistakenly cried he was bleeding to death. Poor fiddler Marion Sumner wasn't as lucky, for he had broken his collarbone.

Chet Atkins left the band to try his luck in Cincinnati. When the war ended in 1945, Johnnie and his bandmates accepted an invitation to play WPTF-Raleigh, where Johnnie and Eddie helped pioneer a brand new *Carolina Barn Dance*. Chet, let go from his stint at WLW-Cincinnati, called Johnnie, who hired him back in the band at WPTF.

At war's end, Jack Anglin was mustered out in early 1946, and Johnnie welcomed him back into the act in Raleigh. Wright had to cut back on costs, however, so Eddie departed for Memphis, this time to work with Ira and Charlie Louvin, and Chet heeded a call to work with Red Foley on WSM's *Opry*.

Speaking of the Opry, Johnnie & Jack auditioned and was hired to join the WSM cast in 1947, after recording for Sid Prosen's Apollo Records in New York City, where with Eddie Hill they cut twelve sides, four featuring Hill's lead vocals. Kitty wasn't part of that package, either in New York or on the *Opry*, which didn't want a solo girl singer at that time. The duo departed WSM early in 1948, with their band now renamed The Tennessee Mountain Boys.

It was four years later that Johnnie & Jack finally found the song and style that set them apart from other "brother" acts - "Poison Love" - which they came across while working on KWKH-Shreveport's *Louisiana Hayride* (1948-1951). It's success also got them back on the *Opry*.

While recording several so-so songs under a new contract with RCA, Johnnie & Jack started singing "Poison Love," when bassist Ernie Newton suggested they do it with a Latin beat, which he created with an assist from Eddie Hill on guitar. The result was phenomenal, giving the duo a brand new Latin flavor to their tracks, resulting in back-to-back Top 10's "Poison Love," "Cryin' Heart Blues" and "Three Ways Of Knowing." A few years later, they hit upon another unique sound, adapting R&B songs to a country beat, scoring number one "(Oh Baby Mine) I Get So Lonely" (1954), followed by yet another smash cover of an R&B hit, "Goodnight, Sweetheart, Goodnight," peaking at number three.

Kitty Wells got her chance for both a hit and an invitation to join the WSM *Opry* cast, thanks to an "answer" song "It Wasn't God Who Made Honky Tonk Angels," spontaneously recorded May 3, 1952, "for the session fee." Decca Records' Owen Bradley produced, backed by Johnnie on bass, Jack on rhythm guitar, along with Shot Jackson, on steel guitar and Paul Warren on fiddle, in Nashville's Castle Studio. Her song was a female reply to Hank Thompson's smash "Wild Side Of Life," and shared a melody with that number, as well as "I'm Thinking Tonight Of My Blue Eyes" and "The Great Speckled Bird." Troy Martin had brought it to Decca's Paul Cohen, and nobody thought it would hit.

Initially the *Opry* management objected to Kitty's debut hit, which hit number one six weeks, claiming it had objectionable lyrics, but Roy Acuff went to bat for her, and she joined the Opry in September 1952. " . . . Honky Tonk Angels," sold a million records, crossed over into the pop Top Twenty chart as well, and made Wells the first country female to chalk up a number one record.

She wasn't a one-hit wonder, following up with a succession of hits, making her Nashville's first female superstar. A decade later, "Pretty Miss" Norma Jean, who cut an RCA album of Kitty's songs in tribute to the *Queen of Country Music*, said, "I was fourteen when I heard Kitty Wells sing 'It Wasn't God Who Made Honky Tonk Angels.' It was Kitty who proved a woman's place could be on the jukebox and on the airwaves."

Sadly, on March 7, 1963, Johnnie lost his partner of twenty-five years, Jack Anglin, who died in an auto accident while on his way to funeral services for his friends Cowboy Copas, Hawkshaw Hawkins and Randy Hughes (who died in a plane crash with Patsy Cline two days earlier). The following Saturday at the *Grand Ole Opry*, heads bowed for a moment of silence, to honor these stars.

According to Steve Eng in his book "Satisfied Mind," Kitty Wells left WSM in 1964. The reason why is one of country music's unsolved mysteries. Kitty and Johnny continued traveling the road, but after sixty years decided to retire on New Year's Eve, 2001. Kitty and Johnny lived a brutal travel schedule, and Kitty was eighty-one, and Johnny eighty-six, when they retired. Kitty charted over eighty-four songs in her career. In 1976, she was inducted into the Country Music Hall Of Fame. Upon retirement, Kitty lamented, "What we have on radio now is not country. They call it country, but it's not." Kitty died July 16, 2012 at age ninety-two, nearly ten months after husband Johnnie's death on September 27, 2011, at age ninety-seven.

Many Kitty Wells' fans remember that she owed her career start and stage name to her early champion Lowell Blanchard, and his *Mid-Day Merry-Go-Round* and *The Tennessee Barn Dance*.

"I shall never forget the day / When we together roamed the Dell / I kissed her cheek and named the day / That I would marry Kitty Wells . . ."

Myrtle Euton.

Kitty in the 1965 film 'Second Fiddle To A Steel Guitar.'

A young Roy Acuff

DOWN MEMORY LANE

Carl Smith in 1948, when he played bass for the Shelton Brothers (from left), Curly Shelton, Benny Sims, Hoke Jenkins, Jack Shelton and Carl, barely out of his teens.

The Cowboy Copas Band

The Don Gibson Band

In the late 1940s, Chet Atkins – and Anita
Carter - toured with Mother Maybelle &
The Carter Sisters, and in performing
shows on WNOX's Tennessee Barn Dance.

Here's Carl Smith after
chalking up hits such as
'Mister Moon' and 'Hey, Joe.'

More recently, Sunshine Slim (left) with former WNOX performers
Jerry Collins, Homer Harris, Tony Mosco and Charlie Pickel.

96

Bessie & Red Murphy headlined WNOX in 1952, along with (from left)
Luke Brandon, Howard White and Blackie Lunsford.

Not sure if this quilt was being auctioned to WNOX Merry Go Round audience or what? But Lowell Blanchard's there along with Tony Musco, Carl Story, Luke Brandon, Jack Shelton and Howard White, way back in 1951.

Here's Jumpin' Bill Carlisle hitting a real high at WNOX-Knoxville.

Jason (Rowdy) Cope checks out a guitar in the Ciderville Music Store.

This photo features a female trio, unknown to this author, at WNOX with backing musicians Blackie Lunsford, Howard White and Sed Addis.

At Cove Lake show, Russ Rickard snapped this shot of Doyle Sowers (from left), Jerry (Chicken Man) Isaacs, Red Harrison and David West in February 2016.

This vintage Chevy pick-up parks at Ciderville, carrying a sign plugging the music.

The pick-up also boasts its own promotional pig, embossed as 'A Hog For Business,' while a posted sign in the rear proclaims: 'This little pig went to Ciderville.'

PART THREE

THE MUSICIANS AND OTHERS . . .

"Without music,
Life would be a mistake."
Friedrich Nietzsche

25 THE MUSICIANS AND OTHERS...

Dobro, fiddle, banjo, guitar, harmonica and piano are traditional instruments. The sidemen and their leaders are really the instruments of music. They put the charm on country music. The musicians who accompany the main event, the sidemen are just as important as the stars. There were also people like songwriters and record men, who hung out at WNOX for promotional purposes. All these people were important to *The Mid-Day Merry Go-Round* and *Tennessee Barn Dance* performers.

In this book are just a few that walked in and out the doors of station WNOX. Sometimes a fiddle player like Chet Atkins starts to play another instrument like guitar and becomes a star performer.

Roy Acuff was just a fiddler in a band, until he recorded "The Great Speckled Bird," which took him to star status in Nashville and beyond. Ellen Muriel Deason was just another singer, until Lowell Blanchard inspired Johnnie Wright to give her the stage name Kitty Wells and she later recorded " . . . Honky Tonk Angels." Then there was Earl Scruggs, who became famous in the Bluegrass world.

Once a guitar player, Jackie Phelps, asked a room full of entertainers who didn't want to give the sidemen a raise, "Where would you be without us?" The star needed the musicians to make them sound great, as much as the sidemen needed the work and paycheck from the stars.

In this part of the book are just a few of those musicians, who dedicated their lives to accompanying artists, but they and all the others who graced the stage at both *The Mid-Day Merry-Go-Round* and *The Tennessee Barn Dance* deserve recognition.

> "*We play our songs and play our old guitar*
> *And it doesn't really matter where we are*
> *When it's time for us to move along*
> *We go where we sometimes sing about in songs.*"
>
> Willie Nelson

Hack and Clyde Johnson, with Ira and Charlie Louvin at WNOX, circa 1946.

26 THE TWO TONYS...
CIANCIOLA AND MUSCO

One of the most delightful people I met while at Ciderville in June 2015 was Rita Cianciola Holder. Although Rita was too young to perform on *The Mid-Day Merry-Go-Round*, her brother Tony Cianciola and her double first cousin, Tony Musco, both played accordion on WNOX's *Merry-Go-Round* and *Tennessee Barn Dance.*

Rita and Tony's mother and father were born in Sicily, just off the coast of Italy in the Mediterranean Sea, arriving by ship at Ellis Island in New York Harbor. Mr. Cianciola discovered Knoxville, choosing to live and raise his family there. He first sold produce, then opened a restaurant, and later became a policeman. Rita, although younger than her talented brother, re-membered her family always loved music. She became the only singer and dancer in the family. Neither her brother nor her cousin sang, but they were both musicians. Her brother played "by ear," while their cousin read music.

In the Fall of 1942, Tony on ac-cordion and Tommy Trent, on guitar, joined *The Merry-Go-Round* house band. Musicians, being musicians, they always had fun to relieve the monotony. It seems that beautiful girls came to see the performers ev-ery day, sitting in the front row and making eyes at the particular mu-sician they liked. Tony would slip girls into the station at night. Once he got so involved, he forgot that the engineer left the building after the last show and locked the door. When

Tony Musco in April 1946.

Tony and the girl realized they couldn't get out, they panicked. Finally they crawled out a back fire escape. When the couple finally got down, they were both black. The fire escape, built right over railroad tracks, had accumulated twenty years of soot and smoke. (Locomotives were coal-fired in those days.)

Rita also remembered a funny story her cousin Tony Musco told her. He said, "When Carl Story sang 'I Found A Hiding Place,' drummer Jerry Collins would 'goose' Carl with a drumstick, when he hit the high note on 'hiding . . .' The word came out *'h-i-iii-ding place.'* " (According to Tony, they did keep it subtle.)

Growing up, Rita came to know the performers the two Tonys' knew, including Archie Campbell and Chet Atkins. When he was a star on *Hee*

Haw, Archie even invited Rita to sing, and Chet, who later ran RCA-Nashville, once told her she had the qualities to become a singing star. Rita also had other friends in Nashville like producer-songwriter Tommy Hill at Starday Records, and promoter Charlie Dick (Patsy Cline's widower), who helped turn Red Sovine's "Teddy Bear" into a number one hit.

Tony with Tommy Trent in 1950.

Although the stars seemed to line up just right for Rita, she chose to stay in Knoxville with husband Raymond Holder. She met David West in the late 1970s, and worked a lot of shows with him, including the Fairgrounds and *A Tribute To USA* show in Maynardville, Tennessee, July 4th. She now sings at Ciderville on Saturday nights. Rita said, "David is a good man, he shares my love of music and dancing. Ciderville is clean and open, no drugs or alcohol allowed."

104

27 JIMMY ELROD...

James W. Elrod was born in the hills of Jackson County, near Granville, Tennessee, July 19, 1939. His family moved to Newport and Morristown, and in high school "Jimmy" played in the school band. But Jimmy loved the sounds of hillbilly bands he heard on the radio, and knew early in life that he loved the banjo.

When he got a banjo, his grandmother, Lerra Estelle Marion Burgess, taught her grandson his first chords. From that amateur start, Jimmy began teaching himself, but would become one of the finest of the East Tennessee crop of banjo pickers.

Probably his first public performance was at WCRK-Morristown. The show, heard every day at 4:30 p.m., was sponsored by Cas Walker's Cash Stores. It featured Tex Climer, Howard Chamberlain, Jim Swatzel and Jimmy. He and those same pickers worked at WATE-Knoxville on a weekly show, also sponsored by Cas Walker. Another sponsor was Blue Band Coffee, accounting for the musicians calling themselves The Blue Band Coffee Boys.

For a short time, Jimmy left Knoxville to play the WWVA-*Wheeling Jamboree* in West Virginia, with Charlie Bailey's band. He returned soon to work at WNOX with Lowell Blanchard on both the *Mid-Day Merry-Go-Round* and *Tennessee Barn Dance,* with Jack Shelton & His Green County Boys. While there, Sonny Osborne taught him to play the banjo backwards, a feat that astounded everybody.

In August 1957, Johnny Masters heard Jimmy play on *The Merry-Go Round* and recommended him to Wilma Lee & Stoney Cooper in Nashville. Their banjo player, Johnny Clark, had left, so Elrod left

Jimmy Elrod steps up to the mic with Wilma Lee Cooper.

Knoxville to work for the Coopers on WSM's *Grand Ole Opry.*

One night at WSM's *Friday Night Frolics,* Jimmy spotted his future wife, Carolyn Underhill. For her part, Carolyn explained, "When I heard him pick, I fell for him!" A mutual friend got them together for their first date, and eventually they were married. One night, out on the road with Wilma Lee & Stoney Cooper, Jimmy called Carolyn and told her he was quitting. He just couldn't take the road anymore. But for a time, Jimmy played with Bill Monroe's Blue Grass Boys.

Thereafter, Jimmy worked at various jobs, in a service station, at Gates Rubber Company and finally for Peterbilt Trucks, where he retired after thirty-one years' service. All that time, he only played banjo for family and friends. The ring of Elrod's banjo was stilled the night of October 15, 2009, when Jimmy died of a heart attack.

28 LOIS JOHNSON . . .

Lois Johnson was born May 15, 1942 in Union County, Tennessee, daughter of Iretta (Butcher) and Fred Johnson, and raised in Maynardville. By age eleven, she was performing on WROL-Knoxville radio, including *Cas Walker's Farm & Home Hour*. When Lowell Blanchard introduced her on WNOX's *Tennessee Barn Dance*, he exclaimed, "She's just great!" Of course, she also performed on the *Mid-Day Merry-Go-Round*, and later the WWVA-*Wheeling Jamboree* (West Virginia).

Lois recorded for Columbia, MGM, Polydor, and 20th Century Records, which released her 1975 self-titled album. Of the twenty singles she charted, Johnson's highest *Billboard* chart song was Don Silvers' "Loving You Will Never Grow Old," which peaked at number six in 1975; and her longest charting record, "Come On In And Let Me Love You," a Top Twenty also written by Silvers, hung in there nineteen weeks.

Lois also hit the charts with Hank Williams, Jr., thanks to such Top Twenty MGM duets as "So Sad (To Watch Good Love Go Bad)" in 1970, and "Send Me Some Lovin'," in 1971. She toured with Hank (1970-'73), and they cut two albums together: "Removing The Shadow" (1970) and "Send Me Lovin' And A Whole Lotta Loving" (1972). Johnson also was a regular on the Ernest Tubb syndicated TV series from Nashville.

Michael Breid, from Eureka Springs, Arkansas, who worked with Lois on WNOX, noted on the *Steel Guitar Forum*, "(Lois) was one fine entertainer. She hit the stage runnin', and the audience loved her. One super gal to work with, always hitting the stage running."

One of Johnson's last studio albums was "Loveshine," released by EMH Records in 1984; however, K-Tel (the TV marketer) released a retrospective in 2002, titled "Country Love Songs." Lois Scoggins Johnson died at Vanderbilt University Medical Center, Nashville, on July 7, 2014, at age seventy-two. Fans of Lois Johnson, recalling her beautiful vocals, feel she deserved far more credit than she got.

29 PETE KIRBY ...
Bashful Brother Oswald (Os)

There weren't any TVs, movies or other conveniences where Pete Kirby grew up in the Great Smoky Mountains. "Os" remembered there weren't any roads from where he lived to what is now Gatlinburg, Tennessee. They rode mules in order to get anywhere.

The Kirbys first lived in a two-room log house. They finally added two more rooms because of the arrival of so many children, eleven in all. The Kirbys slept on mattresses filled with straw from the oats and wheat after the thrashers came through their rural area. Water was carried from a spring and the creek was used to wash clothes on a scrub board with lye soap. Life in general was hard.

When road building began across the Smokies, Os worked on these trails, helping with the survey from the top of bluff mountains to Kentucky and back to Pigeon Forge, and for the highway that was built from Knoxville to Pigeon Forge.

Os's dad ran a singing school, taught back then by old shaped notes, or what was called Old Harp Singing. His sister, Allie, played guitar and sang and went with her dad, when he taught singing. She also had a beautiful, alto voice.

One day, Mr. Kirby and Os decided they would start moonshining. Mr. Kirby went to the Sheriff and told him he was about to lose the farm. He needed a still to make whiskey in order to bring in some money. The sheriff gave Mr. Kirby a still and said to make all the whiskey he wanted, provided he would never let the sheriff catch him in action. Finally, Mr. Kirby became a barber in Sevierville.

Os learned to play banjo and guitar but, at the time, making moon shine seemed more profitable. Os's first real job was at the Johnny Mack Saw-Mill in Sevier County. Os helped Dad make moonshine, before going to the mill to work. Os once worked at the Appalachian Cotton Mill in Knoxville.

Kirby left home in 1929, hitchhiking to Flint, Michigan, but before he could get a job the Great Depression hit. He survived by playing music, the banjo and guitar, at home parties and square dances. At a party, Os met Rudy Wakiki, who was playing Hawaiian music. Os loved Rudy's style of music, and tried to learn what he heard Rudy play. Os never read music, and played totally by ear. He wanted to sound like Rudy, but needed an Hawaiian guitar in order to get that sound.

He moved on to Harvey, Illinois, playing with Roy Brown in beer joints. The bar across the street was drawing huge crowds, because Os's bar owner boss said, the band played Hawaiian music. To keep his job, the next day, Kirby bought an all-steel National Guitar, and began playing it immediately. That was the beginning of Os's stylized music. After a time in the Chicago area, Os went back home, flat broke.

Then something positive happened. Kirby heard Roy Acuff on WNOX-Knoxville. One night when Clell Summey wanted the night off, he told Roy about Pete Kirby. Acuff invited Os to play with him then, and further from time to time. Os played with Roy on *The Mid-Day Merry-Go-Round*. Then Roy left WNOX to go WSM's *Grand Ole Opry*. After three months, however, the guys who had originally gone to the Opry with Roy, left him. Roy drove back to Knoxville and offered jobs to Os, Lonnie (Pap) Wilson and Jake Tendal, offering twenty-five dollars per week.

That was 1937, and they all took Roy up on his offer. Once in the studio, when Acuff and the band were recording "The Precious Jewel," Os suffered an attack of asthma and couldn't hold the notes. He asked the boys to wait, left the studio, found a liquor store, bought a quart of whiskey and in one effort drank over half its contents. He then went back to the studio and finished the record without any problems.

Kirby gave Roy Acuff credit for everything he had in life, including his nickname Bashful Brother Oswald. Os said, "Roy was never a boss. He was just one of the boys." Roy furnished Os with a car to drive until 1966, then he sold him a Pontiac station wagon for one dollar.

Os's memorable laugh set him apart from other artists. Legend has it that some fans came to Acuff's shows just to hear Os laugh, and they felt cheated without a horse laugh, that is if the show ended without hearing that laugh from Bashful Brother Oswald.

"*I'll tell you a story of a Dobro playing man / Well, he's a member of a great country band / I know he's country when he touches the strings / Just listen and you can hear that old Dobro sing.*" - James R. Sullivan.

In an interview for the *Knoxville News Sentinel* in 1983, Os proclaimed, "Country music is just as good as it ever was. Some of them folks don't play it like I do, but then they haven't been at it as long."

30 RED KIRK...
'The Voice of the Country'

Claude (Red) Kirk was born in Knoxville on May 24, 1925. Later, he called himself "a country boy from Wolf Hollow." That was actually his mother's old home-place in Anderson County, Wolf Valley, where the family moved to when he was nine years old.

Dismal Creek ran through the valley, emptying into the Clinch River. Sporting red hair and freckles, it was only natural he was nicknamed "Red." He grew up listening to country, big band music, and the *Grand Ole Opry*. But his very favorite music was heard on WWL-New Orleans on Sunday nights, listening to beautiful waltz music by Wayne King or crooning by the likes of Bing Crosby and Perry Como.

Red grew up sort of under his mother's thumb. She called all the shots and he counted on her doing all the thinking. When he was five years old, mom took him to WNOX to perform on a talent show in the Andrew Johnson Hotel. Red sang "The St. James Infirmary Blues" and won the contest. He was fourteen, when Red's mother took him back again, and this time Lowell Blanchard took a shine to Red. Blanchard liked what he heard, but told Red he needed to develop some vibrato in his voice. A country boy, Red didn't know what *vibrato* was, but as he matured, nature solved that problem.

Kirk taught himself to play guitar, though he first started playing on a Dobro that belonged to a cousin. Whenever cousin went to work, Red would sneak in and practice on the instrument. He started playing guitar after that. While in South Clinton School, a lady came in to teach students guitar, but she taught one lesson, then left town. All Red remembered learning from her was a B-7th chord. He already knew E and A. He liked E because it was the best key for him to sing in.

Red was drafted into World War II in 1943, seeing action with the 37th Division in the Pacific. Upon returning stateside, he went to then Camp Campbell, Kentucky (now called Fort Campbell), and was assigned to a recruiting trek through the Midwest at different fairs and such to entertain. He says that's how he developed his skill to entertain audiences.

In 1947, his service behind him, Red was invited by Lowell Blanchard for a guest spot on *The Tennessee Barn Dance*. He put Red on an off-the-air show, while Eddy Arnold's *Purina Show* was on the network. An off-the-air show was live, just for the people in the studio auditorium. That's when Archie Campbell was doing his Grandpappy character. When Archie went back to his dressing room, Lowell Blanchard told him, "Archie, there's a fellow out there I want you to hear sing, but don't try to hire him, because he's too damn smooth."

Archie went out on stage and listened to Red. Afterwards Archie asked him if he could sing parts. When Red told him he could, Archie asked him to sing in his trio. Red wanted that job and took it. They played *The Mid-Day*

110

Merry-Go-Round and *The Tennessee Barn Dance*, and left immediately for a show in Rogersville. Sunshine Slim Sweet was with them and Smokey White, a fiddle player. Archie said, "I guess we ought to talk money, They don't pay me anything for *The Merry-Go-Round* or *Barn Dance* . . ." (In a short while, Red found out that was a lie. They didn't pay much, but they did pay Archie a stipend.) Continuing, Archie added, "Lowell keeps us booked five nights a week. I'll pay you five dollars a night."

Though Red's heart sank, he worked for Archie for a long time. Finally, Archie let Red sell a picture for twenty-five cents with a few songs he was singing on back. Red made more selling pictures than he did from Archie.

In 1949 when Hank Williams' million-selling revival of a 1920s' song "Lovesick Blues" was proving a smash, Homer & Jethro told Red, "There's a record by Hank Williams you need to learn." So, Red started singing it on shows, and Murray Nash, Mercury's A&R man, asked Red one day, "How would you like to have a record contract?" Red immediately replied, "Where do I sign?"

Red recorded his cover of "Lovesick Blues" for Mercury at WCRK-Morristown, one Saturday night in April 1949, after the *Barn Dance*. For the session, he borrowed Homer's J-200 Gibson guitar because his old arch-top Harmony sounded like someone beating on a damned lard can, as Archie put it. Anyway, that's how Red got on Mercury, which wanted a cover record on Hank's monster single on MGM. Kirk's version stalled at number fourteen on *Billboard*, charting one week - June 25, 1949 - while Williams' spent sixteen weeks at number one, during forty-two weeks' charting.

Red's subsequent sessions for Mercury at Herzog's studio in Cincinnati boasted Jerry Byrd playing steel, Louie Innis on rhythm guitar, Zeke Turner playing lead guitar, Tommy Jackson playing fiddle and Red Turner on bass. In 1950, Kirk fared somewhat better, scoring a Top Ten country hit with Hal Miller's "Lose Your Blues," charting seven weeks.

After leaving Archie's employ, Red became a solo act at WROL-Knoxville for a short time. When continued success on Mercury eluded Kirk, he flitted from label to label seeking success, but never hit the big time again.

For awhile it looked like Red would reach stardom, making appearances on the *Merry-Go-Round,* KWKH-Shreveport's *Louisiana Hayride*, WLS-Chicago's *National Barn Dance* and WSM-Nashville's *Grand Ole Opry*, and he certainly had made important music connections, but somehow subsequent deals all turned cold.

Red wasn't any luckier as a songwriter, lacking real commercial success. He wrote "Wreath On The Door Of My Heart," a Cowboy Copas cut, but *Billboard's* reviewer labeled it too morbid. Things looked brighter in 1961, when Leroy Van Dyke recorded his ballad "My World's Caving In," which looked like an A Side, but DJ's all flipped to the other side of the record, "Walk On By," another smash, nineteen weeks at number one, out of thirty-seven weeks on the chart. Of course, he did make money, just by being on the B side of a much-played record.

"I've always said since then, if you can't be talented and write the hits, just be lucky and get on the back of them," mused Kirk.

Ultimately, Red landed back in East Tennessee, in Kingsport, where he was DJ on a small radio station, and also helped sell cars. The people of Kingsport loved him and they filled the small venues where he and a band played occasionally. The *Voice of The Country* - his nickname - was finally stilled in May 1999.

According to Red's son Chris Kirk: "Red Kirk was my father. He indeed did TV spots for a local Chevy dealer, and we also had Chevy stores and Buicks of our own in the 1970s and '80s. He passed in May 1999, after living his last years in Kingsport, where my mother (Ruthie) still resides (as of 2007)."

Red Kirk with friends Arthur Q. Smith and Howard White, WNOX, 1951.

31 GEORGE 'SPEEDY' KRISE...

As a young boy, Gorge Edward (Speedy) Krise liked to sing and write songs. When he was fifteen years old, he needed an instrument in order to accompany himself when he sang. So, he borrowed a Dobro from a boy, who was courting his sister back in his West Virginia home.

In Hinton High School, Speedy got his first taste of success when he won a talent contest performing "Hilo March," playing the song on Hawaiian guitar, backed by sister Irene on Spanish guitar. A fellow named Tom Ball taught Speedy basics of playing Hawaiian guitar (and later wed Irene).

After graduating high school in 1940, Speedy formed a band, The Blue Ribbon Boys at WJLS-Beckley, West Virginia, traveling to bookings in his DeSoto automobile. There he met Molly O'Day, Roy Acuff and Little Jimmy Dickens.

Jimmy and Speedy were eating a chicken dinner together at the Krise home on Sunday, December 7, 1941, when they learned that Japan had bombed Pearl Harbor. So Speedy enlisted in the Army Air Corps during World War II.

Upon being discharged, Krise moved to Knoxville, where Molly O'Day invited him to go on WNOX with her, playing *The Mid-Day Merry-Go-Round* and *The Tennessee Barn Dance*, along with the likes of Roy Acuff, Carl Smith, The Carters, and Mac Wiseman.

Krise has been cited as the first musician-songwriter to play Dobro on a commercial bluegrass recording. He did just that for a Capitol Records' session with Knoxville's own Carl Butler (while in Butler's band, 1950-'51) on the tracks "Heartbreak Express" and "Plastic Heart," both written by Krise.

Speedy has recalled the time that he and Archie Campbell were working in Tampa, when they heard a young singer from Memphis, rehearsing. They wondered if this raucous entertainer would ever make it as a headliner. Well, that newcomer was Elvis Presley, who literally launched rock and roll.

King of Country Music Roy Acuff also recorded Speedy's song "Plastic Heart," while reportedly Carl Smith made his session bow singing Speedy's song "No Trespassing." Others who recorded Krise songs have included Don Gibson, Jim & Jesse and Mac Wiseman.

In yet another memorable event in his career, during December 1946, Speedy accompanied Molly O'Day to Chicago, where Columbia's Art Satherley produced her first session at the WBBM radio station. Besides Molly and Speedy, the session players included her then-band members Lynn Davis on guitar; Skeets Williamson on fiddle; and Mac Wiseman on the walking bass. (Of course, Lynn was her husband and Skeets her brother.) That's when she cut the classic "Tramp On The Street."

Finally, Speedy quit show business in 1956, mainly to get off the road, but found sales work with the Cook Coffee Company in Akron, Ohio. Now

113

and then he played festivals and such, sometimes with good friend Glenn Lehman, but confided, "I was glad to leave the music business behind."

George (Speedy) Krise died on June 9, 2011, at age eighty-nine, and is buried in the family plot in his home-town of Hinton, West Virginia. Surviving Speedy was wife Freda Mae, a son, three daughters and lots of grand-babies.

You know the word "Dobro" means *good* in the Slavic language, and when it came to playing this unique instrument, the innovative Speedy Krise was among its best practitioners, and he's the player credited with introducing it into bluegrass music. That's about as good as it gets.

32 RAY R. MYERS...
"World's Famous Armless Musician"

It all began on January 2, 1911, on a farm near Lancaster, Pennsylvania, when a boy was born armless to Mr. and Mrs. William Myers, the fifth child in a family of nine. He grew up using his feet in place of his hands. He began walking as any child and by the time he was two years old, he could feed and dress himself. When he was three, he was offered a job in a circus, but his parents refused, wanting him to grow up normally.

Ray R. Myers entered high school at Allentown, Pennsylvania, and graduated with honors. He played trombone in his high school band, studied art and bought himself a Hawaiian guitar. He learned to play, using his feet. With the toes of his left foot, he held the steel bar to note the guitar and with his right foot, he held a very small pick to strum the guitar.

Myers was offered his own weekly radio show on WGAL-Lancaster. It was on this program that Cowboy Loye first heard him, and arranged for Ray to appear on the WWVA-*Wheeling Jamboree* in West Virginia, with him. This gave Myers an opportunity to perform for a wider audience.

Early photo of Ray Myers pickin' guitar with his toes.

In 1933, Ray contacted Robert Ripley and the *Believe It Or Not* show. He stayed with Ripley at the World's Fair in Chicago, until the fair closed. Ray used to keep money in his shoes. If he wanted to use a pay phone, he would kick off his loafers, reach with his toes to get a dime and put it in a pay phone.

When he returned from the World's Fair, and with money he had saved, he bought a small car. He passed his driver's test and the patrolman who gave him his test said, "His driving is perfect." He would kick off his right shoe, pull forth a key, insert it in the lock and slowly start driving. He drove seven hundred and fifty thousand miles in twenty states, never having an accident.

Ray's radio career began on WGAL, but WWVA was the springboard that opened other doors on radio including WMNN-Fairmont, West Virginia; WEEU-Reading, Pennsylvania; WHAS-Louisville; WSVA-Harrisonburg, Virginia; WKBN-Youngstown, Ohio; and on WVOK-Birmingham's *Dixie Jamboree*. Ray worked with such acts as Uncle Jack Nelson, Radio Dot & Smokey, and Cousin Emmy. People turned out just to watch Ray, as he played old-timey music. They called him the "Armless Musician Who Leads A Normal Life."

Ray proved a great performer, and audiences loved him. He was at WNOX's *Mid-Day Merry-Go-Round* for a while. The routine was that a stagehand would bring out his steel guitar, with his picks and bar, to the stage in front of the mike. Stoney Stonecipher, then a steel player there,

115

remembered that one night the band thought it would be fun to cover Ray's bar with Vaseline. Poor Ray, of course, couldn't hold the bar with his feet. Stoney said, "I didn't think it was funny, but the band did."

Myers never seemed to stay long at any one place. The late 1940s found him in Nashville doing shows with Big Jeff Bess, a fixture at Germantown Inn and on WLAC. Some people turned out at Big Jeff's shows simply to watch Ray play, just as they had in Knoxville.

Billy Robinson, then playing steel with Big Jeff, said that he remembered Ray well. He said Ray wore half-socks on his feet with his toes exposed. He wore a ring on one of his toes and a watch on an ankle. Billy said Ray was a real nice guy and remembered him singing old time country songs as he played. Billy said Ray didn't do anything fancy, just using about four chords. The wonder to audiences everywhere was that Ray could do the things he did.

Billy said that one day Ray went to the Department of Motor Vehicles to get a Tennessee Driver's License. The man there said, "You can't drive. You don't have any arms." Ray replied, "Is there a law against it?" . . . Ray got his Tennessee Driver's License.

In 1948, Myers began broadcasting on WLAC-Nashville with co-star Jack Henderson. They were on five days a week at 5:15 every afternoon, sponsored by Gloria Flour Company.

By 1953, Ray was appearing daily on WPDX in Clarksburg, West Virginia. On July 3, 1969, he played at a drive-in theater in Manchester, Kentucky. As far as is known, that was his last performance.

Ray Myers died in Gordonville, Pennsylvania in May 1986. However, he left us a book he co-authored with wife Eleanor Jane, "Ray R. Myers – World's Famous Armless Musician – His Life Story As Told In Words and Pictures." He dedicated it to his mother, who with the help of God gave him his start in life; and the late Cowboy Loye, who gave him his chance for radio fame; and to his radio friends. He and Eleanor Jane, whom he wed in December 1937, were parents to son Ronald, born in 1938 (with all his limbs intact).

Ray Myers signs an autograph for a fan with his feet.

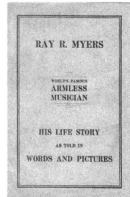

RAY R. MYERS

WORLD'S FAMOUS
ARMLESS
MUSICIAN

HIS LIFE STORY
AS TOLD IN
WORDS AND PICTURES

Ray Myers' biography
(Art work courtesy the
Joe Lee New River Ranch
Collection.)

33 MURRAY NASH...

Robert Murray Nash was born March 5, 1918 in Campbell, Nebraska. By the late 1940s, he was residing in Knoxville and became responsible for the growth of the business of country music. Murray was not a native of East Tennessee, neither was he on WNOX's *Merry-Go-Round* or even a musician, but thanks to his love of country music, he put country music on the road to success.

In 1938, the C. M. McClung & Company in Knoxville, was one of the largest wholesale distributors in the south. McClung wanted to handle RCA instruments, and in order to swing the deal, agreed to put in an RCA record department. They hired Nash to build a real record department at McClung's. His success at this was phenomenal, and he turned it into a real bona fide RCA distributor's department. In three years, McClung had become the number one RCA distributor in the U.S., and the first ever for RCA, below the Mason-Dixon Line.

Until Murray Nash came along, the record business was conducted from a small space on dime store counters that displayed a few records. Nash first built a real record department at McClung's. Never before had a store devoted any real floor space to a record department. Experts said this was the craziest idea anyone ever had. Nash ignored such warnings and went on with his project. He put in shelves and listening booths and ordered plenty of records. His success was assured. Nash went after big accounts all over Knoxville and sold them on the idea of putting in record departments in their stores. Then Nash branched out to other major cities. By the late '40s, McClung's now had a bona fide RCA Victor distributor department. The RCA president in Camden, New Jersey, could not believe what was happening "down there with those hillbillies."

WNOX was a frequent stop for Nash. He had become a force in hillbilly records. He broadened his influence when he became a producer for RCA records, long before Chet Atkins came to RCA. He produced Redd Stewart, Pee Wee King, Charlie Monroe and Cliff Carlisle. Nash claimed he originated the idea of Nashville's Disc Jockey Convention in October 1952. He masterminded the first radio mail-order record warehouse, which became Randy's Record Mart in Gallatin, Tennessee. Nash then helped Randy Wood, owner, to start Dot Records. Dot became one of the most successful independent labels ever, with Pat Boone, Jimmy C. Newman and Mac Wiseman on its roster. After that, Nash helped establish the first one-stop service where jukebox owners could buy all their records in one place.

Eventually Nash left RCA and produced records for Mercury. Then he played a role in the development of Flatt & Scruggs, recording the duo at radio stations in Tennessee and Kentucky for Mercury. He oversaw the label from a Knoxville base at first. One day, Bill Carlisle walked in and sang Nash his novelty number "Too Old To Cut The Mustard." Nash didn't waste time; he signed Bill to a contract immediately. They cut "Too Old To Cut The Mustard" in July 1951. They used a studio that Nash had constructed in Nashville. It was the first publisher's recording studio in Nashville, located in Fred Rose's garage at 3621 Rainbow Trail. Martha Carson, Cliff Carlisle and Chet Atkins, all *Merry-Go-Round* artists, were on that session. "Too Old To Cut the Mustard" hit the charts big that year, and in January 1953, Bill's follow-up "No Help Wanted" scored number one. Those successes also brought Bill to the *Grand Ole Opry* in 1953.

Nobody knew that Carlisle would be the last artist that Nash would ever sign to Mercury. D. Kilpatrick took his place. CONELRAD (Control of Electromagnetic Radiation) was the first early warning system of AM Radio for the public at large. WSM didn't always stay on the air for twenty-four hours. Nash went to see station executive Jack DeWitt, and told him that WSM could have CONELRAD, if they stayed on the air twenty-four hours. Then, thanks to Nash, DeWitt brought Eddie Hill from Memphis to do their first all-night show (which incidentally promoted the Opry).

Murray Nash and Howard White at 1989 WNOX Reunion.

Nash knew all the country D.J.'s and was a tireless promoter of country music, because he really believed in country music. He was proud of it in the days when it was subject to ridicule. He lived country music day and night.

Nash always enjoyed the *Mid-Day Merry-Go-Round* Reunions they used to have. Tony Musco, former accordion player for the show's house-band, was the glue that held it together. Bill Carlisle was always there, as was Howard White. Nash, who never forgot his ties to Knoxville, was always there.

In 1958, Nash retired from the music industry to work for the Post Office in his later years. He died at age eighty-two on April 17, 2000. Murray Nash remained one of those unseen powers behind the stars for many years.

34 ARTHUR Q. SMITH...
'Mystery Man of Country Music'

Arthur Q. Smith was born James Arthur Pritchett on December 9, 1909, in Griffin, Georgia. He hitched-hiked his way to Knoxville in 1936, with a guitar and a suitcase of songs he had written. He did odd jobs and worked as a bellhop at the Andrew Johnson Hotel, hoping for a chance to audition for the *Mid-Day Merry-Go-Round*. Within a month, he was hired as a rhythm guitarist for the house-band. He created the name he became known as, Arthur Smith, using his stepfather's last name, Smith, and his own middle name, Arthur.

Smith earned a little recognition for his own songs at WNOX that he sang on the *Merry-Go-Round* and the *Barn Dance* boasting that hillbilly sound. When another songwriter, Arthur Smith, at WBT in Charlotte, North Carolina, had a hit song with "Guitar Boogie," WNOX held a contest to give their Arthur Smith a middle name. A local Knoxvillian wrote the letter "Q" as an entry, and won.

WNOX gave Arthur Q. a fifteen-minute live show known as *The Tennessee Cornshucker*. He used it to promote his songs. He left WNOX for a short while, serving as a soldier in World War II, then returned to Knoxville and started writing songs again.

Arthur Q. Smith (James Arthur Pritchett) at WNOX, 1951.

You might say that those were the Wild West days of country music. Songwriters were often looked on as second-class citizens in the business and were used mercilessly. Smith would sell his songs for as little as five-to-twenty-five dollars each, sometimes fifty dollars. He also had a drinking problem and sold his songs to entertainers, who put their own names on his songs as if they had written them. There are many stories about how certain "users" knowing his weakness for drink, would put him up in a hotel and buy him liquor, while he churned out song after song. Arthur Q. was said to be a major source of songs for performers at the *Mid-Day Merry-Go-Round*.

Among hundreds of songs he wrote and sold were "Wedding Bells," credited to Claude Boone; "Rainbow at Midnight," credited to Lost John Miller; and "Daddy, When Is Mommy Coming Home," credited to Ernest Tubb and Troy Martin. Those who bought and made hits out of songs of Smith's read like a Who's Who of entertainers: Carl Story, The Carter Family, Don Gibson, Johnnie Wright, Hank Williams, Carl Smith, and many others.

When Smith signed with Acuff-Rose as a songwriter, Hank Williams, Sr., even hired him as a business manager. Smith's love of drinking and Hank's similar weakness was something Audrey Williams would not tolerate, so she fired Smith.

On March 22, 1963, Arthur Q. Smith died from cancer. He was found dead in a flophouse at the corner of Vine Street and Summit Hill Avenue in Knoxville. He left behind countless receipts for songs he had sold. Harlan Howard, the great country songwriter, wrote a song he dedicated to Smith, "Be Careful Who You Love." Hank Williams, Jr., recorded it and it is on his album, "Pure Hank." In 2001, a London magazine called Smith the "Mystery Man Of Country Music."

"He overlooked an orchid, while searching for a rose . . . " and so did we.

35 FRANK SMITH...

"Take a look at the mountains above me
Take a look at the sea deep and blue
Take a look at the valleys below me
All this beauty reminds me of you."

Frank Smith

Frank Smith, one of eight children, was born on what is called the "quiet side of the Smokies," Rockford, Blount County, Tennessee.

Frank's interest in music began when he first heard Cowboy Copas sing the song "Signed Sealed and Delivered." Then he took an interest in Ernest Tubb, Eddy Arnold, Carl Smith, Hank Williams and Faron Young. Frank's interest grew as he sang along with his favorite artists' 78- rpm records. One time, in the third grade, he was asked what he wanted to be when he grew up? Without hesitation, he said, " I want to be a country singer."

Although he knew he could sing, he never sang in public until he was in the Army. While stationed in Alaska, he was pushed into singing. Frank said, "They seemed to like it and I loved it. The more shows I sang on, the more I liked it."

Frank began singing in public after he got out of the Army and returned to Knoxville. His sister-in-law asked him one day to let her try to get him on *the Mid-Day Merry-Go-Round*, but Frank said no. He said, "They wouldn't let me on with all the accomplished singers they have on there."

His sister-in-law kept on asking him to let her try to get him on the show, until Frank finally told her to go ahead and see what she could do. She asked Lowell Blanchard to please put Frank on the show and the next thing he knew, he was singing on the WNOX *Merry-Go-Round*. That first night he remembered a band member said, "Man, he sounds like Marty Robbins." Three of the band members that played that night were Jerry Collins, Tony Musco and Duke Harkleroad.

That was the real beginning of music for Frank. He was also booked on the *Tennessee Barn Dance*. He stayed until the shows closed. He met a lot of people while on the shows, Lois Johnson, Kirk Hansard, Johnny Shelton, Roy Sneed and L. E. White. When Frank was on the *Tennesssee Barn Dance*, Lowell Blanchard introduced him as the "Mayor of Halls Cross Roads." (Frank lived near Halls Cross Roads.)

Frank recalled that Lois Johnson would go on the show right before him and she always sang the song he was going to sing. He would have to change songs on the spur of the moment. One night he asked her why she always went on stage and sang what he planned to sing. She told him she was so sorry, but from then on, she always checked with him and they never had that problem again.

One night Lowell came to Frank backstage and said, "You're as good as anyone I ever had on this stage, but you have to work on your timing." Frank said he followed Lowell's advice and worked on his timing, but still messed up sometimes.

When Lowell Blanchard's shows came to a close, Frank stayed on with the *Tennessee Valley Barn Dance* with John Hitch. This kept him close to Knoxville. Frank also did shows around the Tennessee area, like the *Lafollette Jamboree*, David West's *Cider Barn* and the *Barn Dinner Theater.* He also visited Nashville, writing songs and "pitching" them to artists like Red Sovine and Marty Robbins. He recorded songs for RCA with producer Bob Ferguson, and for Pete Drake's Stop Records. Some of the musicians who played on his records included Pete Drake, Jack Drake, Jerry Smith, Johnny Gimble and D. J. Fontana. The engineer was Scotty Moore. Frank said: "I never quit going to Nashville, I just didn't go as often as I should have."

Frank was on a lot of shows with a lot of big names. Once he fronted a show for Jim Ed Brown and was supposed to have been on the bill with George Jones, but "no show Jones" didn't make it. He was scheduled to do a show with Sonny James, but Frank didn't show up; however, he did play on shows with the likes of Jack Greene, Claude Gray, Norma Jean, Wayne Kemp and Bill Phillips.

Frank has been all over the country singing, but these days he likes being around Knoxville with wife, Doris, and seeing their grandchildren grow up. He still stays involved in music, singing at such places as David West's Ciderville. He also sings for various charities and benefits to help others. He also authored a book, "The Roads I've Traveled (And The People I've Met)." Singing is still an enjoyment for Frank Smith. He said, "I have been up and down that road, and I'd do it all over again, if I could – except for a thing or two.""

"We will reach old age at last
And look back upon the past
And I'll have the sweetest love
A man could ask."

Frank Smith

36 STONEY STONECIPHER...

When William (Stoney) Stonecipher moved to Knoxville, he lived at 961 North Fifth Street, just down the street from Kitty Wells and Johnnie Wright, and across the street from Carl and Pearl Butler.

Stoney began working with a local band, The Country Kings. He was glad to be there. In those days, Knoxville was the place to be. He had started out playing mandolin and guitar. When in school, he had played with a local school band and at a practice session, started playing another guy's steel guitar. Then he got himself a Gibson laptop steel. (Must have cost at least $150, according to Stoney.)

"Like all other steel players at that time," said Stoney, "I wanted to sound like Jerry Byrd did on his seven-string Rickenbacker."

Stoney began working on the *Mid-Day Merry-Go-Round* and *Tennessee Barn Dance* with Red & Bessie Lou. One day backstage, he met Charlie Monroe, who asked him to sing tenor with him. Stoney said, "Charlie was easy to get along with," and added softly, "Not a thing like his brother, Bill."

When Stoney was at the *Merry-Go-Round,* its roster included The Carters, Carl Story, The Davis Sisters, Eddie Hill, Flatt & Scruggs, JamUp & Honey, Kentucky Slim and Lois Johnson.

Stoney went on the road with whomever he could work with. Once with Bill Carlisle, he agreed to go on a day when three shows were booked. He got in this huge Chrysler with five guys, all their instruments, and a big bass fiddle. Their shows were in Morristown, Lenoir City, and Sweetwater. Of course, they had to make time between dates, but when Stoney looked at the speedometer, it read one hundred and five. It scared him to death, going that fast on a two-lane road.

Stoney was still at the *Merry-Go-Round* and *Barn Dance* during the move to Willow Springs. One day, a man from Golden Crest Recording in New York heard the *Barn Dance* and asked if he could record them. Permission was given and they brought all their heavy equipment down from New York to record. They recorded a "live" album. On that recording were Stoney, L. E. White, Luke Brandon, Johnny Shelton, Jerry Moore and the Dyer Sisters.

The Merry-Go-Round and *Barn Dance* didn't survive the Willow Springs move for a lot of reasons. According to Stoney, TV had come on the scene, and people just didn't want to go as far out as Willow Springs, and Lowell Blanchard was successful in his own little world, and just didn't want to get bigger.

For some thirty-five years, Stoney was playing and emceeing shows for the International Steel Guitar Show in St. Louis. That was a great time and the turnouts were tremendous. Unfortunately since DeWitt "Scotty" Scott died in 2014, those sweet steel guitar tones are heard no more in St. Louis. Stoney Stonecipher, however, still plays and can usually be heard playing pedal steel guitar at Ciderville on Saturday nights. Time marches on.

37 CLELL SUMMEY . . .
(Cousin Jody)

The Lord must have intended for James Clell Summey, (a.k.a. Cousin Jody), to be a comedian or he wouldn't have let him be born in a place called Possum Hollow, Tennessee. He was always a comedian as well as a musician. Clell was born about 1913 in the Great Smoky Mountains. As a child, he moved with his family to Knoxville. Mom and Dad were musicians, who recorded on cylinders and Edison discs.

Clell loved the guitar and when he started playing he discovered that when the ring on his finger hit the strings, he got a wondrous sound. That was the start of his steel guitar sound. He switched to the Dobro, and by 1931, was playing his own Hawaiian show.

As a member of the Tennessee Crackerjacks, which began while playing with a group that hung out at George Steven's Arlington Drug Store or Thompson's Garage, he shared the stage with Roy Acuff, Jess Easterday and Bob Wright, and they got a program at WROL-Knoxville, sponsored by Dr. Hamilton, a dentist.

After a short time, Lowell Blanchard talked them into going to WNOX on a new show, the *Mid-Day Merry-Go-Round*. The program was on every day, except Sunday, beginning at noon. One of their guests on the show was Pete (Oswald) Kirby, who would later join the band. Eight months later, they went back to WROL and became known as the Crazy Tennesseans, adding bassist Red Jones to their line-up.

Acuff went to the Opry in 1938, taking along Easterday, Summey and Jones, and changing the band's name to The Smoky Mountain Boys. Clell became the first musician to play Dobro on the Opry stage. His playing is also heard on Acuff's classic recording of "The Great Speckled Bird." About November 1938, Clell and Red became increasingly restless and uneasy because Roy had decided to "croon" and play pop music. They disagreed that the future of the band lay in the Opry with old-time hillbilly music. Clell and Red abruptly quit and returned to Knoxville on January 1, 1939, where they returned to play hillbilly, and Oswald succeeded Clell in the Smoky Mountain Boys.

Clell continued to make personal appearances. In 1945, he was playing with Pee Wee King as a Golden West Cowboy. He played an electric guitar, shaped like a guitar except it had a hollow body and a hole. He could play it without plugging it in. Then he was drafted into the Army. (Don Davis, steel guitarist, took his place.)

After the Army, Clell made many television appearances and several movies as a comedic act, "Cousin Jody & His Country Cousins." He became known for playing his "biscuit board," as he called his Gibson lap-steel guitar. He returned to the Opry as Cousin Jody & His Country Cousins, who were Kitty and Smiley Wilson. He also performed with Lonzo & Oscar, and did a comedy duo Odie & Jody for a time, teamed with Oral (Cousin Odie) Rhodes.

As Cousin Jody, he recorded on Starday Records, and his most popular records were "Television Set," "Mr. Farnsworth's Rooster" and "Lady Cop."

Cousin Jody, Clell Summey, became the ultimate rube comic. He blacked out his teeth, wore baggy pants, sang comedy songs and even though a great Dobro player and steel guitarist, played his old biscuit board, making people laugh. Summey died of cancer in 1976.

38 SUNSHINE "SLIM" SWEET ...

SEABEE, SINGER, SONGWRITER

Sunshine "Slim" Sweet was a *Mid-Day Merry-Go-Round* regular. His given first name was Harley. He was a most prolific musician, who joined the Burchfield Brothers, but left soon to join Molly O'Day's band. He was front man for Molly, but departed to join Archie Campbell and Red Kirk in a new vocal trio, performing at WNOX.

He served the Navy in World War II as a Seabee in the 24th Construction Battalion in the Pacific. In 1949, Slim signed with Mercury Records in Nashville. He recorded his "I Just Told Mama Goodbye," which was covered by Hank Williams. Hank later told him, "Slim, you wrote one hell of a song." Co-written with Curly Kinsey, Slim's lyrics bared the pain of losing the one who brought him into this world: *"I've just told Mama goodbye / Mother's Day has turned to night / Like the flowers in May / She withered away / And my red rose is turnin' to white . . ."*

Sweet definitely had a way with words, and he loved to tell stories

about the acts on the *Merry-Go-Round*. His favorite was about Bill Carlisle. He said, "There was a pretty girl working in the office at WNOX. You had to go up a long stairway to get to her office. Bill would tell Lowell he was going up and kiss that girl. Bill would go up there, come running out and slide down the bannister. The girl would run out and throw a trash can at Bill, and it would clatter down the steps. There was a big round wooden knob at the end of the bannister and I always figured one day Bill would hit it, but he never did. I also wondered how Bill could stand flatfooted and jump up on that five-foot high stage as he did."

Sunshine "Slim" Sweet lived in Heiskell, his home since he was four years old. Mainly he played guitar, and was the last surviving member of the *Mid-Day Merry-Go-Round*, who played until he passed away, May 30, 2011, at age ninety-two.

In almost identical poses: Sunshine Slim (Mama's Little Hillbilly), at WNOX in younger days . . . and (right) more recently Slim at Ciderville's Music Store.

39 BONNIE LOU & BUSTER ...

The First Couple of Down-Home Entertainment.

Bonnie Lou (Margaret Bell) and Buster (Hubert Moore) gained fame playing country, bluegrass and gospel music, with careers spanning from the 1940's to the 1990's. They met when Buster was on the radio with the Carl Story group. Bonnie was in high school. Buster went into the service and when released, Bonnie had graduated from high school. They married in 1945.

Buster, an accomplished mandolinist, had a band at WROL with Cas Walker's show. When one of the boys became ill, Bonnie Lou filled in for him. She became so popular that Buster kept her on as a permanent member of the band. Then he changed her name from Margaret to Bonnie Lou. He thought it was a better stage name. Buster organized his band with Bonnie Lou, Lloyd Bell (Bonnie's brother), Carl Butler and Art Wooten, becoming The Dixie Partners. They traveled from town to town all over the Southeast, playing on any radio station they could connect with.

In the early '50s, theirs became one of the first live television shows for WJHL-Johnson City. Later, Bonnie Lou & Buster became regulars on Knoxville's WBIR-TV and WATE-TV, while constantly touring. In 1963, they began performing on *The Jim Walter Jubilee*, sponsored by Jim Walter Homes. Bonnie Lou did the commercials, extolling the virtues of Jim Walter's custom and modular homes. They remained on the show twenty-one years, until it went off the air.

Since most of their Jim Walter shows were recorded, in 1972 they created their *Smoky Mountain Jubilee,* during the tourist season, in the Coliseum at Pigeon Forge. Performing with Bonnie Lou & Buster were David West, banjo; Lloyd Bell, singer; Little Roy Wiggins, steel guitar; L. E. White and Ava Barber, vocals. (Ava would become a featured singer on *The Lawrence Welk Show.*)

It was on the *Smoky Mountain Jubilee* that they started bringing in the cloggers from North Carolina. There was clogging every night. The show featured bluegrass, as well as country and gospel. Buster liked bluegrass, so they always had a banjo. David West played banjo for years. The old programs list West as playing songs like "Blackberry Blossom" and David Earl's "Breakdown." L. E. White sang "Company's Comin'." Even Scotty Stoneman was on the show sometimes, as was singer Mel Street.

In 1968, a fifteen-year-old girl, Brenda Carter, was working with Bonnie Lou & Buster at Pigeon Forge. She got an offer to sing with George Jones. Being so young, George hired her father as bus driver, so a parent could accompany her. She and George recorded "Milwaukee, Here I Come" and "Great Big Spirit of Love," for which Brenda and George are credited as writers. This was just before Tammy Wynette began working with George.

128

Bonnie Lou & Buster were not quite bluegrass. They had a country sound, more like Molly O'Day, but they didn't imitate anyone. Their music was top notch, their humor unapologetically cornpone. Over the years they never deviated from their original plan, to bring old time variety to the stage, radio and TV. The Coliseum closed their show in 1995 and Bonnie Lou & Buster retired. (Buster died in 1996.)

Their only connection with the *Mid-Day Merry-Go-Round* was when Buster came home from the service. Bonnie Lou's family wanted her to audition for the *Merry-Go-Round*. However, Bonnie Lou got as far as Knoxville, she met up with Buster again and she never did audition for the *Merry-Go-Round*. They were very popular in the Knoxville area and people watched them and followed their careers for years and years. A fan is likely to say, "I grew up watching (or listening), to their show for years and years." Bonnie Lou & Buster didn't care what went on with the commercial music scene. They did what they wanted to do and did it well. They made music together for fifty years. (The author felt they deserved space in this book.)

40 SPECIAL ADDED ATTRACTIONS...

Curly Seckler – He played mandolin and later became an original Foggy Mountain Boy, performing with Flatt and Scruggs.

Earl Scruggs – He lived in Knoxville, while playing on the *Mid-Day Merry-Go-Round*. When Earl and Lester Flatt teamed up, they became one of the best bluegrass bands anywhere. Later, Earl made a name on his own, leading The Earl Scruggs Review.

Carl Story & The Rambling Mountaineers -- They were a popular band on the *Mid-Day Merry-Go-Round*. Carl went on to become known as the "Father of Bluegrass Gospel Music." He recorded for different labels through the 1970s. He was a fixture on the bluegrass festival Circuit. His band was known as a training ground for many future country artists.

Joe and Bill Burchfield -- The Burchfields were regulars on the *Mid-Day Merry-Go-Round* and *Tennessee Barn Dance* in the late 1940s, performing old-time bluegrass and gospel music. They were musically oriented and earned the respect of music producers with their act. They were signed to Capitol Records in 1947, and the East Tennessee sound they brought to the stage influenced other recording stars in country music.

Red Rector and Fred Smith – They worked together as a team on the *Mid-Day Merry-Go-Round* and *Tennessee Barn Dance*. Rector went on to become a respected musician and was a fixture in Knoxville's music community, until he died in 1990.

Johnny Shelton – He made a name for himself as a local musician. He played regularly on the *Tennessee Barn Dance* and did so again on the revival in 1982.

Homer Harris -- He was known on the *Mid-Day Merry-Go-Round* for the song "Little Brown Jug." He was known as the Seven Foot Smiling Cowboy.

Jess Easterday – He was born in Knox County in 1912. He started his music career in 1930. He entered into radio in 1934, with Roy Acuff's Crazy Tennesseans and was billed along with Clell Summey as "Radio's Famous Hawaiian Duo."

Red Jones -- A skilled bass fiddle player. *The Merry-Go-Round* billed him as the "Bill Fiddler King and Jug Comedian." He, too, worked with Roy Acuff.

Imogene "Tiny" Sarrett -- She joined the Crazy Tennesseans shortly before they left Knoxville. She was known as the "Little Girl With the Big Guitar." She went to Nashville with Acuff, but when Clell Summey and Red Jones left Acuff and went back to Knoxville, "Tiny" returned with them.

Riley Puckett -- He was a trailblazer at the *Mid-Day Merry-Go-Round* in spite of blindness. He was a member of The Skillet Lickers and famous for his version of "My Buddy," "Thompson's Old Gray Mule" and "You've Got To See Mama." He was one of the most recorded hillbilly performers of the 1920s and '30s.

Jack Greene – He was born and raised in Maryville, Tennessee. He played on the *Tennessee Barn Dance* and hung around backstage at the *Merry-Go-Round*, hoping for a chance to join the cast. Once he did do a guest spot. He left the *Barn Dance* in 1948, with a group called Cecil Griffin and His Young'Uns. He did a stint in the Army and then played with The Peachtree Cowboys in Atlanta. He joined Ernest Tubb in 1962, playing drums, making thirty dollars a day. He recorded "There Goes My Everything" in 1966, which went number one, earned CMA Single of the Year, and he was off and running, out on his own. Jack was just another artist from WNOX to hit big in Nashville.

It wasn't all fiddle and banjos. There was a WNOX House Band that played big band music. Musicians at different times were: Billy Bowman, John Gallaher, Tony

Jack Greene

Cianciolo, Tony Musco, Jerry Collins, Dave Dunham, Charlie Hagaman, Buck Houchins, Guy Campbell, Tommy Covington, Hubert Carter, and probably others.

There were also the *Mid-Day Merry-Go-Round* reunions. Some of those attending were: Murray Nash, Jerry Collins, Dave Durham, Tony Musco, Hubert Carter, Troy Hatcher, Bill Carlisle, Red Kirk, Howard and Ruth White and many others. There was always a bond between those who worked at the WNOX shows. There aren't too many left, but when any two met, there was bound to be a reunion of sorts. Life in the business takes one in a lot of different directions.

41 LUKE BRANDON & HOWARD WHITE...

"He's not heavy, he's my brother"

"The road is long
With many a winding turn
That leads us to
Who knows where."

Bobby Scott-Bob Russell

Luke Brandon and Howard White became close friends while playing with Don Gibson at WNOX on the *Mid-Day Merry-Go-Round* and the *Tennessee Barn Dance* in 1952. That year they recorded with Don in Nashville for Columbia Records. Those records didn't hit, the most notable being "No Shoulder To Cry On" and "Sample Kisses." They recorded at Castle Studios in Nashville, located in the Tulane Hotel at Eighth Avenue and Church Street, a block from the WSM studios. Castle was the first and the most popular place in Nashville to record at that time. (In 1956 the old hotel, dating from 1894, was razed for a parking lot.)

Howard White was from Charlotte, North Carolina. In 1948, Howard recorded a demo session for Bill Trader, a songwriter. That demo session produced the song "(Now and Then There's) A Fool Such As I," later a hit for Hank Snow (1952), Elvis Presley (1959) and Baillie & The Boys (1990). Shannon Grayson heard Howard play steel guitar at that session and asked Howard to record with him and the Golden Val-

Luke and Howard, 1958.

ley Boys in Cincinnati on King Records. In 1949, Howard again recorded with Grayson on RCA in Atlanta. Then in 1950, Lowell Blanchard at WNOX asked "Daddy John" Love from Charlotte, to sing and yodel on *The Tennessee Barn Dance*. Love then took Howard along to play steel guitar. They rode a Trailways' bus to get to Knoxville and back to Charlotte. They could ride free, as Love's brother-in-law was one of the Trailways' owners.

132

Howard was back home in Charlotte when Don Gibson, who had heard him at the *Barn Dance* called and asked Howard to come to Knoxville and play steel for him. Don's steel player, "Eagle Eye," was going back to school. It meant that Howard would be working at the *Merry-Go-Round, Barn Dance* and any of Don's road shows. Howard did not own a car, but caught a ride to Knoxville with a friend, who drove a chicken truck.

When Howard first went with Don, the band was made up of Sed Addis, guitar, Blackie Lunsford, fiddle and Billy Kirby, bass. Then Luke Brandon replaced Addis on guitar and Marion Sumner replaced fiddler Blackie Lunsford. Occasionally, Howard and Luke played at WROL with L. E. White, Roy Sneed and Ralph Cornish.

Luke Brandon, East Tennessee's most respected guitar player, began playing ukulele at age five. His father, Luke Brandon, Sr., played guitar for The Roane County Ramblers, a highly regarded string band that recorded in the late 1920s. Luke, Jr. received his first guitar, a small bodied Martin, when he was seven. It wasn't long until he began playing music with his father at schoolhouses and political rallies. Luke was only sixteen when he auditioned for Lowell Blanchard at WNOX, with a guitar and vocal act. Blanchard gave Luke a five-minute slot on the *Mid-Day Merry-Go-Round*.

Howard made a lot of friends while at WNOX: Bill Carlisle, Chet Atkins, The Carters, Martha Carson and Archie Campbell, all who later moved to Nashville. One of Howard's best memories was when Archie Campbell invited him to his home for Thanksgiving dinner, since he was alone and had no place to go.

Howard and Luke's friendship remained all their lives. As they grew older they liked to talk about the old days. They remembered that one time on the road with Gibson in Kentucky, they had car trouble. There were no cell phones in those days, and Howard walked to a farmhouse to make an emergency phone call. The nice lady let him in and then he saw a pig in the house. Howard said, "That was the prettiest pig you ever saw, like the one on the CBS-TV show *Green Acres*. The lady talked to that pig like a member of the family." Howard thought that strange, even in Kentucky.

Howard and Luke recalled a trip with Bill Carlisle to Jackpot, Nevada, about twenty miles from Nevada's northern state line. On the way, the car kept blowing tires. Dottie Sills, a singer, was with them. Every time they blew a tire, she laughed hysterically. By the time they got to Jackpot, they were riding on four new tires. That ended Dottie's fun.

Don Gibson was easy to work for, according to Howard and Luke. They recalled he was a real hypochondriac, always going to the doctor. For a while, he even wore a football helmet in the car, in case of an accident.

By 1952, Howard, Luke, and the band were doing great with Gibson at WNOX, but then Lowell Blanchard, wanting to help Don save money, talked Don into putting the band on salary for thirty-five dollars a week. That cut them from the eighty-five dollars a week they had been earning at the WNOX shows, at road dates, at a club on Highway 52 and at square dances at Chilhowee Park. The whole band quit, and Billy Kirby joined the Army.

The band was working the last night of their notice at the *Barn Dance* when the phone rang backstage. Howard answered it and the call was from Randy Hughes in Nashville, who was then managing Cowboy Copas. They needed a fiddle player for an upcoming tour. Howard told them that Marion Sumner was available, and then said, "Could you use a guitar player and a steel guitar player?" Randy replied, "Yes, y'all come!" So, Howard, Luke and Marion all left Knoxville and went to Nashville to go on tour with Copas, a name artist.

None of the boys had a car and they didn't have enough money to get to Nashville, but Howard had saved three-hundred-and-fifty dollars in the bank. With that money, he bought a 1933 Ford sedan. The three of them, and Luke's wife and kids, started out, dropping off Luke's family in Rockwood. They had to stop frequently to add water to that old car. It smoked and boiled all the way to Nashville. They spent the night at the Sam Davis Hotel, meeting Randy and Copas there the next day. That began a seventeen-day tour. They left that old car at the hotel and Howard never went back for it.

Neither Howard nor Luke had ever been on a tour like that, seventeen one-nighters, each date about seven-hundred-and-fifty miles apart. Mostly they slept in the car, rotating drivers. There were no Silver Eagle buses in those days and no super highways. As soon as they packed up from one date, they drove to the next. After that tour, Luke and Marion quit, going back to Knoxville. Howard stayed in Nashville with Copas.

Howard lived at Mom Upchurch's boarding house in East Nashville, and whenever Luke was in Nashville, he stayed there, too. As years passed, Howard and Luke worked many shows together. Although Chet Atkins used Luke on sessions whenever Luke was in town, Luke just never stayed very long in town. East Tennessee always pulled him back. Howard stayed in Nashville and when Copas disbanded, he eventually worked with Wilma Lee and Stoney Cooper, Hawkshaw Hawkins and Jean Shepard, Minnie Pearl, Hank Snow and, as it's said in show business, "many others."

In 1953, while Howard was with Copas, he wrote some instrumentals. Copas liked them and introduced him to Fred Rose, co-owner of Acuff-Rose Publishing. Rose liked the songs and recorded Howard on his Hickory Records label. Howard, of course, called Luke to record with him. Also on that session was Grady Martin, guitar, and Strollin' Tom Pritchard on bass. They recorded in Rose's garage at 3621 Rainbow Trail. Two singles were released from the session, "The Dove," backed with "Ensonata" and the "Steel Guitar Swallow," backed with "Rosette." Those instrumentals were mainly played by DJs when they came on the air or in closing their shows. They were good records. How could you lose with the great Luke Brandon on the session! As *The Pickin' and Singin' News* reported: "Popular Nashville Sideman has first record release. Howard White, one of WSM *Grand Ole Opry's* leading sidemen, is now a recording artist in his own name . . ."

After Luke left Knoxville and went on that tour with Cowboy Copas, he decided he didn't like life on the road. Even though playing with Copas would have led to being on the Opry, along with Howard, he passed that by and decided to go back to Knoxville and the *Mid-Day Merry-Go-Round*. The Carlisle Brothers then hired Luke to play guitar with them and Luke played with Bill and Cliff from 1953 to 1955. Luke recorded on "I Need A Little Help" with Bill, the 1953 follow-up song to Bill's 1952 number one record "No Help Wanted."

Luke Brandon always did what he wanted to do, wherever he was. He split his time between Knoxville and Nashville, doing sessions in Nashville when he wanted or going back to Rockwood when he pleased. In 1955, he worked in a steel mill in Rockwood. Then he got a call from Archie Campbell, who invited him to become a member of the house band on *Country Playhouse*, Knoxville's first TV country music show from WROL.

In the late '50s, Luke spent awhile in Hollywood. There he recorded with Fats Domino and Ricky Nelson. In 1958, he played on the number two hit, "All American Boy" by Bobby Bare. He also played on "When Will I Be Loved" a 1960 Top Ten by The Everly Brothers.

Along about 1964, promoter John Kelly, manager-husband for Judy Lynn, put a band together for her tour in Nevada. Boise-born beauty Judy was Miss Idaho of 1955. Lynn's new band featured Luke Brandon, Howard White, Don

Luke's famed white shirt and tie, in the Ciderville Museum.
(Photo by Kathleen White.)

"Suds" Slayman, Joel Price and Willie Ackerman. She had a Top Ten hit "Footsteps Of a Fool," and played casinos all over Nevada.

One day, Howard was coming out of the Golden Nugget in Las Vegas, when he spied Luke out in front with a crowd around him. Luke was clogging to the crowd's delight. They were even throwing change at him. The band broke up when Judy decided she was going to make her home base in Vegas. None of them wanted to stay in Vegas. Nashville was their home base, so the band returned to Music City. Of course, Luke drifted back to Rockwood.

Howard said, "Luke was one helluva guitar player. He could play rhythm and lead at the same time." Howard also knew that Luke was like a leaf, always blowing with the wind. He was one of a kind. Once Luke was waiting for a bus and looked down and saw some ants. One had a big crumb of bread. Then another ant took it away from him. Luke stomped that ant stealing the crumb and said, "You dirty little bastard!" That was total justice in Luke's mind. Howard said, "Luke could have been the most in-demand guitar player in Nashville, but Luke wouldn't stay here. His heart always took him back to Rockwood and Knoxville."

In about 1965, Luke met David West at the Ciderville *Music Barn*. Luke and David became fast friends and soon Luke started hanging out at David's music store. Luke and Chet Atkins were great friends, starting at *the Merry-Go-Round*. Luke told David that once Chet asked him, "What would you do if I turned RCA over to you?" Luke told Chet, "First thing I'd do is hire some strings like the big bands and change country music completely." Chet sometimes followed Luke's advice and it wasn't long until he began recording Eddy Arnold with strings and Eddy went Pop-Country, leaving off the fiddle and steel guitar.

Luke was a natural-born talent. Bradley Reeves from the East Tennessee Historical Society said, "Luke Brandon was the quintessential East Tennessee musician. He lived his whole life to play and make people happy." Once Luke told David, "It's not Chet's fault I didn't make it with him." David believed him. He knew that Luke did whatever Luke wanted. Once David said, "Luke, you must be a satisfied musician. You make all the musicians around here sound good. You're the best." Luke only replied, "Luke loves ya." Luke was never jealous of fellow performers, always complimenting them. Speaking of himself to the *News Sentinel* in a 2009 interview, Luke said, "I'm just one of those working musicians, who love what they do. Music is something I can't do without."

Luke Brandon today.

I remember Luke best when he used to drive up in his old car to visit Howard and I in our East Nashville home and eat fried chicken. Always, during the time he was there, he would say, "Uh,uh, Ruthie, I just washed my shirts. Would you, uh, uh, mind ironing them for me?" Of course I minded, but I ironed them anyway. This happened every time Luke stayed awhile in Nashville and was headed back to Rockwood. When I visited Ciderville, there was one of Luke's white shirts on display. It brought back too many memories of times gone by.

Howard and Luke went in different directions as the years rolled by, each doing their own thing. Luke never quit being the extraordinary guitar player that he was born to be. After fifteen years on the road, Howard changed careers, staying in the business end of music, and music publishing.

After Luke could no longer make the trips to Nashville, Howard called Luke frequently, always saying, "Lu-lu-lu-Luke, this is Howard." (Howard, for some reason, always started his conversations that way.) Luke always laughed, saying, "Love ya, brother." Luke and Howard always called each other "brother," a common practice among union musicians.

The last time Howard and Luke played together was in St. Louis at the International Steel guitar Convention. Stoney Stonecipher, steel guitarist, was emcee. He said, "Howard talked a lot on stage about the old days. I wanted him to get on with the show as I had a schedule to keep." One of the songs that Howard and Luke played was "The Dove," the song they recorded together in 1953. Although they had not been together in a few years, it was like old home week. They were two old pros playing together again. Howard told Luke, "You play better than ever, brother." Luke replied, "Luke loves ya, brother." When they returned to Nashville, Luke said, "Come on back to Knoxville and let's play Ciderville together." Howard agreed, "Okay, Lu-lu-lu-Luke, we'll do it." It never happened.

Howard died in 2008, after having a dream in which he saw himself and Jerry Byrd playing steel guitar together. He didn't know where they were, but he said it was the most beautiful music he ever heard. (Byrd had died three years before.) Luke left us in 2012. It's a wonder he isn't commuting between Heaven and Knoxville.

"It's a long, long road
From which there is no return
But I'm strong enough to carry him
He's not heavy, he's my brother."

Bobby Scott-Bob Russell

42 THE AFTERGLOW . . .

"Some people come into our lives
And quietly go,
Others stay for a while and leave
Footprints in our hearts....
And we are never, ever the same."

Louis (Grandpa) Jones

History was made at WNOX. For a time, Knoxville's stars surpassed even Nashville's. The *Mid-Day Merry-Go-Round* groomed and developed a whole generation of country music stars. All that ended when its stars were tempted and lured by WSM radio's *Grand Ole Opry* to Nashville. When the major record companies finally decided "Hillbilly Music" had a commercial future, the record industry built permanent studios in Nashville. Then WNOX artists like Bill Carlisle or Carl Smith went to Nashville to record. When their records hit, they were wooed by Opry management, noting Nashville was the place to be. It wasn't necessarily money that lured them. WSM didn't pay any better than WNOX. They had always depended on their road shows to make money, back in those days. It was just so exciting being where all those studios, publishing companies and the Opry were located.

Without the *Mid-Day Merry-Go-Round*, the *Grand Ole Opry* probably would not have become as rich in talent as it became. At that time, WSM was busily building its schedule to suit NBC. The *Merry-Go-Round* became a sort of stepping stone to the Opry. A lot of the greats all played WNOX and WROL first.

In the music business there's always that little word "IF." If WSM had not been owned by the powerful National Life Insurance Company; If recording studios like RCA, Columbia and Decca had not gone to Nashville; If music publishing companies like Acuff-Rose, Tree and Pamper had not been available; If many top musicians had not been so available; If all this had been centered in Knoxville, then their futures could have been made at WNOX, instead of WSM.

In retrospect, I suppose you could say that the *Mid-Day Merry-Go-Round* became a farm team for the Opry. The stars that were groomed by Lowell Blanchard went on to become country legends. The talent on that WNOX show reads like a roll call for the Hall of Fame: Pee Wee King, Roy Acuff, Archie Campbell, Carl Smith, Chet Atkins, Martha Carson, Don Gibson, Kitty Wells, Johnnie & Jack, Cowboy Copas, Mother Maybelle & The Carter Sisters, Bill Carlisle, and oh so many others.

What Knoxville threw away, Nashville made a fortune on. Although Nashville was christened *Music City USA* by WSM disc jockey David Cobb, there was a time when Knoxville could have been owner of that title. Knoxville was well situated to attract performers, who were the real deal. Such artists and musicians not only moved to Nashville, but sometimes moved to places like Springfield, Missouri or Shreveport, Louisiana or Chicago, but WNOX-Knoxville and Lowell Blanchard will long be remembered by music historians for an industry that started it all. Even now WNOX remains a Knoxville institution but alas, not for live country music.

Yes, Lowell Blanchard discovered and paraded a string of performers across his stage, who became stars. He was quoted as saying, "I train 'em and Nashville gets 'em." Blanchard was comfortable with Knoxville being the cradle of country music, instead of the home of country music. Maybe he was right. "Keep it real, keep it country, keep it low to the ground," as the saying went.

All those *Merry-Go-Round* performers made memories every day that have since slipped into history. They were entertainers, but that's not all it was about. They had the feelings of joy and tears, happiness and hurt, life and love. Even though their era has gone, those people who loved to perform on the stage of the *Mid-Day Merry-Go-Round,* need to have their stories told and re-told before they are unheard and lost in time.

There is hope for the music that is real country and low to the ground, for the country music as we knew it has become only a memory. David West, who pioneered a *Music Barn*, has kept it going and it is known today as Ciderville. Yes, David keeps real country music alive there. He has stayed to finish weaving the threads left in the loom. The artists of today at Ciderville are keeping the origins of music from our mountains and valleys relevant. Then there is also radio station WYSH, 1380 on the radio dial, where James Perry and David Farmer keep traditional country music current. Their show is also broadcast on 101.1 FM and simulcast at 960 AM. They are heard as far away as Australia, keeping real country music alive and well. Not to be out-done, David West broadcasts on WYSH on Thursdays, direct from Ciderville.

While the artists from Southern Appalachia may travel to the East or to the West, or they may go North or South, but their hearts feel that relentless pull to return to the place of their birth. Each of us is a link between the past and the future. It is up to us to pass along the music history. Otherwise, the stories, songs and traditions of the Appalachias will be lost. Hopefully, the wagon-load of memories shared in this book have made long-ago artists come alive again and our new ones will keep on singing and playing the music from their hearts.

.

"Oh that my words were now written
Oh that they were printed in a book
That they were graven with pen and lead in the rock forever."

Job 19:23

THE SOUTH . . .

"The place where tea is sweet
And accents are sweeter.
Front porches are wide
And words are long.
Y'all is a proper noun
And someone's heart is always being blessed."

ACKNOWLEDGMENTS:

This book would not have happened without a lot of help from friends. First, I want to express my heartfelt thanks to James Perry of Maynardville, who pointed me in the direction of this exciting ride through the Knoxville music scene.

A very special thanks to David Farmer and David West for their knowledge of musical growth from *The Mid-Day Merry-Go-Round* to Ciderville; and to Faye West for her familial thoughts regarding this era of sounds.

As always, thanks to my daughter, Kathleen for her encouragement, advice and for driving "Miss Daisy" wherever I needed to go. Also thanks to my son Bob for his contributions. I also remember my late husband Howard, for telling me about the times he spent in Knoxville at WNOX with Don Gibson.

There are many supporters of the *Merry-Go-Round* and Ciderville, who have given of their time and knowledge with facts and *reminiscences* of legends along our journey. The time I spent with Rita Cianciola Holder at Ciderville, was truly delightful. Special thanks, too, to Bob Wyrick who remembered all the lyrics to the *Merry-Go-Round* theme song. Also appreciate Frank and Doris Smith, who so generously let me use their book for an inside look at their side of music in the Knoxville area and beyond.

Stoney Stoneciper allowed me to visit with him for hours, while he told me all about his life in music with the steel guitar. Rowdy Cope spent time telling me stories about David West and introduced me to all the pictures on the wall at the *Music Barn*.

I also want to thank Karen Leuthke, Jon Sweet, Bill Paisley, Wanda White Matthews, Oneta Wright, Juanita McPeak, Mac Wiseman, Bob Bean, Luke Brandon, Carolyn Elrod, Billy Robinson, John Simon, Mike Streissguth, Gary Gentry, Shirley Hutchins and Mike Misetich from Texas.

Writing this book would have been impossible without the help of so many amazing people who gave their support, especially David West. He gave freely of his knowledge about the music business. I appreciate his time and hospitality, and the sharing of his musical talent.

I also want to thank Nova Books Nashville and Walt Trott, who always helps me turn my dreams of a book into reality. In sifting through the wonderful world of music through the eyes of all these exciting area musicians, I just want to say:

"Put me on the highway,
And show me a sign,
And take me to the limit,
One more time."

Glenn Frey\Don Henley\Randy Meisner

Ruth White

BIBLIOGRAPHY:

Joel Whitburn's "Top Country Songs: 1944-2005" (Billboard charts); "Not Too Old To Cut The Mustard: Jumpin' Bill Carlisle & Friends Talk About His Life And Country Music Business" by Anita Capps, Over-Mountain Press, 2000; "The Encyclopedia of Country Music," Paul Kingsbury, Oxford University Press, NY, 1998; Wikipedia, The Free Encyclopedia (on the Internet); "Lowell Blanchard: A Forgotten Father of Country Music," Jim Tumblin, 2014, Knoxville; "Tennessee Encyclopedia of History and Culture – WNOX," by Carroll Van West, MTSU, 2009; "Images of America: Knoxville's WNOX," by Ed Hooper, Arcadia Publishing, 2009, Chicago; "Knoxville Tennessee, Cradle of Country Music" by Richard Basch, Smithsonian, Washington, D.C. (Striped Pot, 2011); "The Roads I've Traveled (And The People I've Met)," Frank Smith, Knoxville; "Voices Of The Country" by Michael Streissguth (Routledge Publishing, New York, 2014).

PUBLISHER'S ACKNOWLEDGMENTS:

In addition to the creativity of Author Ruth B. White, Nova Books wishes to extend an appreciative nod to graphics designer-technician Tom Barkoukis of BarkoDesigns, Nashville, TN; Bill Trott, web manager, Phoenix, AZ; Mary C. Haag, transcriptionist, Dodgeville, WI; and Bill Brough, co-editor, Nova-Nashville. A special thank you for providing art work and photography goes to Billy Robinson, Kathleen White, Joe Lee (New River Ranch Collection), Dave Farmer, James Farmer, Rita Cianciola, Carolyn Elrod, Phil Campbell, Mike Misetich, Russ Rickard, Faye West, David West, Mac Wiseman, the late Howard White, WNOX, WROL, WSM, and for photos from W. Trott's private collection. Cover designs by Tom Barkoukis.

ABOUT THE AUTHOR

Ruth Bland White, a Nashville native, began playing piano as a teen in a seven-piece band under the baton of Bill Wiseman. Although their families had it annulled, she and the band's drummer Murrey (Buddy) Harman were married briefly (he went on to become one of Nashville's original A Team session musicians). Ruth, a graduate of East High School, worked at Strobel's Music Store and attended Ward- Belmont College, as a music major. In the store, she played sheet music songs for customers. After moving to Chicago with late husband Bob Kirkham, she managed the music department in a major retail store. Upon returning to Nashville, she worked briefly at Strobel's, where she met future husband Howard White, then a steel guitarist for Opry superstar Hank Snow. Moving on to WSM, she managed the station's music library, assisting Opry stage manager Vito Pellettieri, and the TV show's *Waking Crew* band director Marvin Hughes, with their music needs. In 1965, she wed White, working with him in their Locomotive Music publishing firm, and together co-managed Henry Strzelecki's October Records, an independent label sponsored by Pepsi-Cola. Subsequently, Ruth worked on Music Row for Country International Records, Strzelecki Publishing, Reed Music, Inc., and artist Porter Wagoner, running the Opry legend's production, booking and publishing operations. She has become the *go-to* gal for advice on administering music publishing and copyrights, an expertise sought by such clients as Carmol Taylor, Norro Wilson, Sonny James, Gary Gentry, Charly McClain, Joe Stampley and The Nashville Superpickers (including players Strzelecki, Buddy Spicher, Phil Baugh, Buddy Emmons, Pig Robbins, Terry McMillan, Bill Pursell and Buddy Harman). She was production coordinator on albums involving Canadian vocalist Lucille Starr; White's gospel collection; and a music CD for The Hermitage, a popular tourist site. In 2010, Ruth was the recipient of a SOURCE Award, recognizing her pioneering accomplishments on Music Row. She is mom to Bob, Jr., and Kathleen White. A prolific author, Ruth White's books have included: "Every Highway Out Of Nashville" (JM Productions/Picker's Rest, 1990); "Mecklinburg: The Life & Times Of A Proud People" (JM Productions/Picker's Rest, 1992); "The Original Goober" (Nova Books, 2004); "You Can Make It If You Try," the biography of R&B pioneer Ted Jarrett (Hillsboro Press & Country Music Foundation Press, 2005); "Nashville Steeler," a biography of veteran guitarist Don Davis (Schiffer Books, 2012); and "Every Highway Out Of Nashville, Volume 2" (Nova Books, 2014).

*Country DJ Hall of Famer
Lowell Blanchard.*

INDEX:

146